By Edwin Rosskam
TOWBOAT RIVER *(with Louise Rosskam)*
THE ALIEN *(Novel)*

Edwin Rosskam

ROOSEVELT, NEW JERSEY

Big Dreams in a
Small Town & What
Time Did to Them

Grossman Publishers
New York   1972

Copyright © 1972 by Edwin Rosskam

First published in 1972 by Grossman Publishers
625 Madison Avenue, New York, N.Y. 10022

Published simultaneously in Canada by
Fitzhenry and Whiteside, Ltd.

SBN 670–60751–7

Library of Congress Catalogue Card Number: 78–185018

Printed in U.S.A.

for Louise
and for the settlers and the tenants
and the renters by a tenant.

1

Goldie Rosenzweig is getting old. She's had to stop working at her trade in a nearby garment factory. Now she's on social security and rents a room to our only policeman. When she walks to her son's house to visit her grandchildren, you can tell that her feet are giving out. But she still paints her eyebrows.

Louis, Goldie's husband, had heart trouble and was much respected, as was evident from the turnout at the shul not so long ago, after he quietly died while tending the flowers in his back yard. The two of them and their children were among the first eight families to settle in town.

"We came in 1936," Goldie told me. "The houses weren't finished. The school wasn't finished. The roads weren't finished. Nothing. Only two cars in the whole town. We walked so many times the four miles to Hightstown. We had to go shop. We had to go to the drugstore.

"Some stores wouldn't let you in. In one of them I went to buy something that year. So the man said:

" 'From where you come?'

"I said: 'From Jersey Homesteads.'

"He said: 'I'm not going to sell you.'

"I said: 'Why?'

"He said: 'Because it's communist there I won't sell you.' "

Goldie's eyes are still handsome, and her face is remarkably

I

free of wrinkles. There's not a drop of self-pity in her. Not ever, no matter what happens. It's hard to believe her when she tells me, casually, that when they came, she was a very nervous woman.

"I used to cry every minute," she says. "We didn't make a living. We suffered here. Herman was little and he didn't understand. But Stella was twelve years old, and to take her away from all we had in New York—such a nice place New York was then, thirty-five years ago. Here was mud. Here was dark. It was no life.

"Stella used to sit in a chair days and nights and make pictures, draw hands and faces. No libraries here, no movies here, no friends here, no cars here. Nothing here.

"I said: 'Look, you will get older, you'll grow up and get married. But for papa and for me this is the place. Because you know, when papa gets older, they'll throw him out of any other factory. But not this one. Here the factory belongs to all of us. We'll surely have it for a lifetime.' "

Herman and Stella, Goldie's children, are grown. Herman is an opera singer and married to a pianist. Stella is one of those bright people who can turn her hand to anything: she draws beautifully and writes and does elegant graphic design. She's married to a city planner. Herman and Stella are sophisticated, educated and cultured within the American rather than the Jewish concept of what culture means. Still they returned to their village after the usual outward ventures, with umbilical cords apparently intact.

Stella speaks for both of them when she recalls what it was like for a child to move out into the open country from the crowded city.

"I remember the times when we would take trips out here to see the land and the foundations," she says. "And I remember we left Manhattan in buses, and I was torn between this wish to disassociate myself because I didn't even want to look as though I were with these people—on the other hand I had this enormous loyalty to them because there was a newspaper reporter on the bus from the *Journal American*. I remember him sitting in the back. I felt very protective of the people because I sensed how he was viewing my people from the outside without knowing their true qualities.

"But mixed in with this general set was a great deal of phantasizing that had to do with living in a little house and going to a country school. It was a totally literary idea, like the Bobbsey Twins and the Andy Hardy movies or whatever else was around at the time. For instance I was very hot then on getting a sweater set where you had an underneath sweater and a top sweater. And I wanted a red one and I was thrilled to see myself in this outfit in this country school, having this kind of very American experience.

"You must understand that in the city I didn't know anybody, except two girls whose mothers spoke English well. Everybody else spoke and thought in Yiddish. The school wasn't Yiddish. The teachers were mostly Irish, so that the school appeared to us pretty much as I imagine the Negroes feel about school now. One had to protect one's customs against the teachers, because, while they might discuss the joys of Christmas, you were made rather ashamed of the joys of Hanukah. We learned English, it's true, but we would have learned that anyway.

"I don't know whether you can imagine the impact of an open space on people who had been born then in the crowded parts of a city. I was acutely uncomfortable in the country. I might have been put on the moon in terms of its visual and feeling impact. I was used to the security of all those packed bodies around me. And so much space, all of a sudden, is just as frightening as sleeping in a room by yourself when you never have. The quiet, the lack of light, the sense that there is nobody packed around you . . . I felt this the first evening I was here. I took my little brother for a walk. There was only this one street built, and we two children walked down that street. All the lights were on in the houses, and all the windows glittered. I had never seen such a display of glass behind which was human habitation, not stores. And somehow I got a sense of tremendous beauty, not because of the beauty of the surroundings, but because I was overcome by the beauty of the vulnerable idea and the people groping for it, and the fragile bravery of these people whom I knew to be fragile.

3

"Every child has a very exact scale in him of the relative strength of his family in relation to the world of his community. You see, the world around us then was the depression. And although I knew that personally my father wasn't fragile—not at all, he had always impressed me with his energy in fighting his fragility—he was a Jewish father. And around me in the city were Jewish fathers dying of leadpoisoning, Jewish fathers out of work, Jewish fathers helpless. And so on that first night, walking with my brother and seeing those windows, I was moved to tears. I really remember the tears streaming down my face because my father and his friends had succeeded in producing this glittering thing against all those odds I knew existed, but couldn't have articulated then."

*

By the time my wife and I bought our house in 1953, Jersey Homesteads had given up its name. It was now called Roosevelt, New Jersey, after the father of the New Deal and the leader of the war against Hitler. The change was made, I gather, while the whole nation was in mourning. Even some of those who hated him grieved, since grief comes cheap after the book is closed and the man is dead.

Here in town, I believe, the sorrow was genuine: the change of name was accomplished simply and without show, by a unanimous action of the Borough Council. But I don't really know. The act is in the minutes, but I can't tell what the town felt like at the time, since I wasn't here. And this, obviously, would mean a lot more than any item that can be written down in the records. That's why I'm no scholar, probably, because I believe in the feel of things and in the stories people have to tell rather than the facts that are only bones.

As Ben Shahn used to say: "Most facts are lies; all stories are true."

One fact, however, I can vouch for: No two of the people left over from the beginning (informants they are called, aren't they?) agree on any fact more meaningful than the date when the town was founded.

And even this—you might think that this date would be easy

to establish. It's on any number of documents, and the newspapers covered the story. The difficulty is, where do you want to count from? The day (or night, more likely, since night is usually considered the propitious environment for visions) when Benjamin Brown (whose real name is supposed to have been Lipshitz) dreamed up the project? Like other dreams, this one is hard to pinpoint. Or do you want to start with the more extended period when a committee of prominent philanthropists, advised by Brown, tried unsuccessfully to found a colony of Jewish farmers? Or the time when the U.S. Department of the Interior (where Brown had connections) reluctantly agreed to build his co-operative dream project, where immigrant Jewish tailors from Poland or Russia were expected to work part-time in a co-operative garment factory and part-time on co-operatively managed farms?

Not that it matters much whether you count from 1934 or '36. The depression was at its worst—so hopeless that little hopes like this one were allowed to grow in odd places—and that matters. The settlers were immigrant and Jewish, and that matters. They weren't yet very comfortable in English and removed from the *stetl* and the pogrom only by their sojourn in the tenements of Williamsburg and the Bronx. And the way those staunch, quarrelsome, socialist-oriented individualists felt and thought about the world and their place in it has proved fundamental to the story of this tiny out-of-the-way community they founded in the big, hostile New Jersey landscape. Even until today.

*

Prejudice is two-sided. But only the big, formless majority has the power to practice discrimination. In the thirties the countryside hereabouts and especially the centers, such as Hightstown, four miles away, were part of the South. The Klan was a fact of life like the bank on Main Street and the potatoes in the fields.

Here's how a teacher at the high school remembers growing up on one of the back streets:

"I grew up in a poor section. There were the railroad tracks," he says, "the traditional divider, and on that side there were homes, and on the other side was a Negro church and Shangle's

Alley. And there were some little restaurants, little shacks where people had fish fries, and there was a big bar in Dawes Court. There were homes of a sort around there too, between there and Rogers Avenue, and Mom Samanowitz had a bar there which catered to about four or five blocks of poor people. And that's where I remember a big cross on fire. I don't know what was the particular reason for it. It was just the climate of the period. It was Mississippi exactly. The whole climate was Mississippi. . . .

"There was no such thing as a revolution of rising expectations. Everybody who was poor rented. The landlord sent a little guy every week for the rent. I remember my father chasing him up the street after the ceiling fell down and hit Mom. You never worried about the heat, they didn't give you heat—but the ceiling! I guess we paid like thirteen dollars a month.

"My point is, you never thought of owning a home. That couldn't enter your mind in your wildest dreams. That was something the people did in another part of town. We didn't think about the other part of town. Any more than a Negro would think of going into Sam Ford's bar. Or a Catholic of going to any except that funny church, St. Anthony's. It was Mississippi exactly."

"And the Homesteads?" I asked.

"The Homesteads," he shrugged, "that was the place for the Jews."

*

The *stetl* is a frame of mind. There is no key to it: not money, certainly, nor shared persecution. You would think that the loss of several relatives to Hitler's ovens should be ample price of admission. It isn't.

To me the Old Testament is a basic myth, the foundation under a faith that once hoped to unite the world. To our old people, to the original settlers, it is *their* book. The roots of their still ardent spirit are sunk deep in The Book; it is what separates them from the rest of the world. Whether they are religious or not makes no difference. The images in their heads grow out of The Book. They can no more take them off than they can take off the flesh from their bones.

6

When we arrived, the number of old settlers had shrunk to a minority more vocal than effective, but still big enough to hold a club over a proposed school budget. A veto, which, incidentally, they could never bring themselves to exercise. They could make a great noise at school board meetings. Some scolded, furiously. Others were ironic, and their words bit. But no school budget was ever voted down. Not in this town. Alone in the booth a grandfather couldn't bring himself to go against his deep conviction that education means survival for a Jew in a universe of anti-Semites.

And now? The attrition of the aging has been so gradual that it passes almost unnoticed. There have been signs, and we could have read them. The shul has stopped paying a full-time rabbi and the orthodox section of the cemetery is filling up. With taxes out of sight, how can a retired garment worker on social security keep living in a four-thousand-dollar house suddenly assessed at seventeen thousand dollars? People move out. Strangers with money are moving in, engineers from RCA, salesmen from big companies, professors from Rutgers. Young people with shiny cars whose children swim in pools behind the houses where vegetable gardens used to be. What do they know of Jersey Homesteads? Not even the name.

Besides, the dank climate of Central New Jersey is bad for arthritis.

Last fall on a gray day Nathan Gratz made the rounds of the homes where he was still known, to say good-bye forever. Under his bushy black brows I could see him hold back the tears. Once the town had been his life and later the source of a deference he demanded and got. He had been the president of the co-operative association which antedated the houses. He had sat on public bodies. Every year at graduation time eighth graders competing for the history essay prize fidgeted in his dim, neat living room, while he realized himself again in his long-winded way, talking solemnly of the historic days when news reporters came to observe a social experiment that might have turned out seminal—except for a few minor mistakes—for the entire troubled nation.

He was the aristocrat among proletarian tailors. In Russia, rumor has it, he had a gymnasium education. Before his wife died, I have been told, pure Russian, not Yiddish was spoken in his home. Nathan was an institution. And now he was leaving.

"Why are you going, Nathan?"

"I have nobody here to talk to."

I got a sense of betrayal from him, a deep, contained anger. Tall and straight and slim, an old-fashioned ladies' man with ink-black hair I am sure he's been dyeing since before I knew him, he's never capitulated to his eighty years. He's had some kind of squabble with the Town Council over something to do with his house, and he lost.

"Where are you going, Nathan?"

"Miami, where I still have friends."

"The town won't be the same without you, Nathan."

It won't either.

*

At the post office where we get our mail, unknown young men, dressed for some business somewhere or bearded in dungarees, are strangers to me in more than one sense: none of them personally remembers National Socialism or the great war or a non-nuclear world.

Maybe we *are* on the way to becoming a suburb.

2

The land around us is fine for crops. Even now, with old roads being widened (not ours, thank God, not yet) and a brand-new divided highway chewing up acres by the thousand; with jerrybuilt, slick developments fitted to the tastes and incomes of junior executives and salesmen (they'll be transferred anyway in a couple of years); with childless senior citizens' communities to the north of us—modern, with air-conditioned bridges over rustic ponds, or colonial and very busy with oversize tricycles and arts and crafts—with all this, wide sweeps remain of wheat bending in the wind, of potatoes and tomatoes in perfect rows aimed at the hedgerows on the horizon.

But no tourists, no. They zip through our main street and past the corn and soybeans, and they haven't been here at all. They don't pause. They don't see. They don't have time.

Not that this country hides its face. It's wide-open, gently rolling, with telegraph poles marching out of sight, sometimes a little crooked, in the pale haze of summer.

What's there to see? Not much for the guidebooks. Though near town there's history, if you must have it, as there is in all places where men have lived. A meeting house with a cannon ball in the old brick wall. The grave—provided you can locate it—of Abraham Lincoln's great-grandmother. And, of course, a battle site. Every self-respecting landscape must own its battle site.

But if you have the time—that's the main thing, time—to walk or bike or slowly drive down a dirt road, you may see wild flowers in the patch of light at the end of the green tunnel through a clump of woods. You might come on a pheasant in an open field, stupid as a chicken, but gorgeous as the king of England at coronation. Or a rabbit skittering away with his white flag high. Or, if you're very lucky, a deer looking at you with big eyes before he crashes into the undergrowth. Even today, yes: only fifty miles out of New York.

And the nights! I'll let Myron Weiss speak about the nights: Myron, who started as a carpenter, which wasn't usual for a Jewish boy fifty years ago.

His mother wasn't the only one who tried to talk him out of carpentry. In Waterbury he went to see a builder about a job.

"We don't hire Jewish fellows," the man said. "All our men are Italians." But Myron insisted.

What made him so determined? Myron remembers.

"It was before we came to this country," he says. "I was working in a distillery. I hated it. Then one day I got into the cooperage shop where they made the barrels. There were men in there cutting and sawing and fitting the rigs around the barrels, and the smell of the oak was terrific. You know the smell of cut green oak, it was terrific. So right there I made up my mind I was going to work with wood."

If you were to meet Myron, you would never think of him as a man who chose his life's work because he thought the smell of oak was terrific. He's a small contractor these days, struggling, but somehow making it, and I guess he doesn't touch wood much anymore except maybe superstitiously, in conversation. He himself looks as though he were carved out of wood or even stone, with big, rough features and simple planes in his face and with prominent veins under his graying, bushy hair. His judgments are uncomplicated and direct: peasants' judgments, essentially, and strictly utilitarian. Yet, in his story of his first night here, well before Jersey Homesteads was conceived, there is a touch of unexpected sensitivity.

"This was in 1930," he says, "and Benjamin Brown decided

to buy a farm here and build a co-op. He'd have poultry and he'd have a dairy. He knew I was a carpenter and he asked me if I would undertake to move out here and build it for him. And I said sure I would like to. Because at that time there was a big depression. So he met me one morning in the early part of June, and he had a Hudson car, and I came out with him. Just to look around. And when we got here Mrs. Brown had the table set, and there were other visitors too.

"So it was that first dinner. That's the most important dinner in my whole history. After we ate I felt like having a smoke and I asked to be excused and went outside.

"It was a moonlit night, and you could actually see the three hundred acres stretched out. Standing on top of that hill, you could see all around you as far as the eye could reach. And the air was full of spring smells: trees and jasmine, different flowers that come from the woods. It was terrific.

"The air was pure and clean, and I was standing away from the house, my back was to the house, and I didn't see Brown come out and stand behind me. All of a sudden he was behind me and he said: 'What do you think of it?'

"I said: 'I'll tell you something, Mr. Brown,' I said, 'whether you're going to hire me or not, I'm not going back to New York.'

"He said: 'What do you mean—just the first couple of hours, and you're not going back to New York?'

"I said: 'That's right.' "

Myron built Benjamin Brown's house and later he helped build the two hundred houses of the town. He's been elected mayor—twice, if I'm not mistaken—partly because everybody knew him and partly, I am sure, because people thought he was hardheaded and practical. But then, of course, the voters had no idea of how he came here in the first place, captured entirely by the quality of a moonlit night.

How did the settlers and their children see this landscape? As soil, commanded to be fruitful? Or as those damned furrows which had to be labored over and which were the source of drudgery and aching bones? Individuals differ about it.

It is therefore proper, I think, to start with the account of

Edward Siegel, a former administrator of Jersey Homesteads. He's a big man now in public housing, and he really doesn't have much invested around here anymore.

"We—ell, you see," he says, leaning back from his impressive desk and sucking on his pipe, "the problem was that—well, you take a guy who's been a union man all his life, and he knows that when he works, he gets a dollar and a half or two dollars an hour. And when he doesn't have any work, he doesn't work. And then you take him out to the field and you expect him to pick potatoes for twenty-five cents an hour, and he has to work a lot harder. He just won't do it. He says: 'Why should I do that? I'll just sit on my backside and read a book . . .' We tried to get the youngsters to do this work, but they wouldn't. The kids weren't interested in the farm either. After the first day or two of picking potatoes they were so doggone tired, they never came back."

The administrator should know. He had the responsibility for the whole project, if not the co-ops. He should be as close to an objective observer as can be found. But his cool statement doesn't agree with Bill Perlmutter's recollection at all.

Bill was a boy at the time, and he and the rest of the local children went to school in a farm community some ten miles away. He remembers working in the fields every day during the harvest. And in his home garden besides. But then, of course, Bill is nostalgic about the whole experience, he has lived it, he didn't see it through a paper sieve of reports and accounts and forms.

"We were the migrants of the time," Bill says. "There were no blacks working in the fields. They didn't need them. They could pay us less wages. Every kid here all summer worked on the farms. On our way home from school the bus would stop at the side of the field, and every kid used to go with dungarees under the seat, and you'd slip into your dungarees and you'd ask a girl to take your books home and you'd go into the field and work till dark. You couldn't afford a trowel to dig with, so you cut a stick for the cabbage. We got about fifteen or twenty cents an hour, and they got their money's worth. After the cabbage you'd cut seed potatoes, and, if you were lucky you'd help plant. And every bit of it went home on the table. And we'd work in asparagus and in the corn fields, pulling the suckers off the corn. And when the potatoes came in everybody picked, and when we knocked off you went home and you finally got something to eat and you grabbed your swimming trunks and your bicycle and you went to Etra Lake and that's where we swam. And if you were very fortunate, they would pay you twenty cents an hour loading bags of potatoes on trucks, and you'd stack them and go to work in the barn, grading them. You had to have a hundred and three pounds in a bag because of the shrinkage, and the bags were sewed up and you loaded them on another van and you went home and you lay down and died. You didn't have time to get in trouble."

Bill is close to forty now, I would estimate, a lean-faced fighting cock of a man, the son of a retired electrician who still lives in town and a cheerful old lady who is famous for her *Mandel Brot*. The family as a whole, but the two men in particular, are known for their bluntness, to put it mildly, in a community where few are reticent: father and son thrive on controversy. Both would feel cowardly if they were ever to call a spade less than a goddamned shovel. They tend to be on the far right of any town issue and they wave the flag whenever the opportunity arises. On the Fourth of July you can see them both, resplendent in their uniforms as members of the Jewish War Veterans, marching ahead of the traditional cheerful parade of kids in fanciful costumes or on bicycles decorated with colored paper. Both are, I am convinced, disguised sentimentalists.

"There was no place to go," Bill says, talking of the old days. "I remember walking these streets and there were no street lights, and it was mud up to your behind. From here to the corner you wouldn't have shoes. When you got there, you wouldn't even know you had lost one. In the morning there was a shoe stuck in the mud. . . ."

That mud is an important piece of everyone's remembering. It is always mentioned. And every year it gets deeper. If Bill lives to seventy, the mud in the stories he will tell his grandchildren no doubt is going to be neck-deep.

"This was a time of sharing," he goes on. "You shared food, you shared everything. If there was spare time in the proper season, the kids went out berry-picking. Everything under the sun

13

went into a jar. My mother made thousands of jars of jam of all kinds, tomatoes, berries, whatever could be made into jam. In our garage we had big bins filled with sand, and we'd bury carrots and potatoes in them, or bushels of apples. Every apple was wrapped in newspaper. Once every thirty days you'd unwrap them, set aside the ones to be eaten right away or made into more applesauce, and then rewrap the good ones. It kept everybody busy. You were always tired. But after New York, for a twelve-year-old kid it was exciting. We had a sense of pioneering."

Pioneering? Does the claim implicit in this American word seem preposterous at this remove in time? Not to me, not quite. Put it in the context of a nation terrified by the prevalence of hunger in the city streets, by farmers dispossessed, by banks shaken to their foundations, as was the whole structure of a people's faith in themselves and their destiny: these immigrants were the pioneers of a new idea, even if their hardships were trivial by comparison with the legend. The little New Jersey settlement, with the hand of a protecting and benevolent government held over it, was their high adventure, their affirmation against the national terror of collapsing certainties. And who's to measure the comparative size of fears and the courage required to meet them?

"Those were the poverty years," Edward Siegel told me. "Most of the people had no way of earning anything. The rent was fourteen dollars and the taxes were eight dollars, and most of them couldn't pay either. The only money they had was the fifty dollars a month they got from welfare. After the factory failed."

The depression is hard to remember even for us who lived through it. For the young it's unimaginable.

As Goldie puts it:

"The younger children can't understand a lot of things. When I look back to years ago, I don't know how we lived and were so happy with what we had, any little comfort, any little thing. So when you see what the children have now and what we had—I don't know. What kind of crazy world is this? When I tell my grandchildren about Russia and I give them the facts, they can't get over it. They can't understand. Here, when we had a warm house and something to eat—even if we didn't have butter on the table—we were happy, singing and everything. Now they throw out more than we were eating then. I gave my children as much as I could. We worked and gave them a nice education. But they knew there were times when we haven't got it. . . . These children of now, they don't want to understand. I say a child has to eat good and have what to wear. But some other things they don't have to have. The stuffed animals, you could make a zoo out of them. I used to make a doll from rags and play with it, and I was so happy with that doll. Now you go out and pay ten dollars for a doll, and they play with it one day. What is that? Everything you can buy now for pay later. I don't know how they live today. I don't know."

NEW DEAL RAISES A LITTLE SOVIET.

This is a headline from a Philadelphia paper of 1936.

The subhead:

Soviet-Inspired Project Near Hightstown to Have "Co-operative" Needlework Factory; Director-in-Chief is Russian-Born.

And below that, in the body of the story:

"200 carefully selected families, headed by a Russian-born little Stalin, will be running their 'co-operative' full blast not 50 miles from the birthplace of American Democracy."

Little Stalin, my eye! Benjamin Brown.

A decent man, an idealist, a socialist of sorts, perhaps. Mainly a believer—in co-ops, obviously, but as much, as far as I can gather, in the idea that Jews would gain dignity by getting their hands into soil. Hands now, roots later, he hoped.

He must have been ridden by the knowledge that in the tzarist Ukraine where he was born, Jews were not permitted to own land. I can well imagine that land and the working of it must have assumed for him—as it had for other American Jews before him—an almost mystical significance.

Russian-born? Brown was Russian-born. And that was enough to make him out a Red in a time when Henry Ford and Gerald L. K. Smith and Father Coughlin hammered daily on the fears of people who were bewildered because they couldn't understand what had happened to their reality.

Not that it matters to me whether Benjamin Brown was a communist or not. It just happens that he wasn't. He was a believer, yes: it takes a believer, a minor messiah (who is so certain of his own rightness he doesn't give a damn about the odds) to make even the smallest alteration in the accepted relations between human beings and property. And I guess, if you measure it with such a yardstick, that's what his dream project was: a very slight innovation affecting no more than a couple of hundred tenement families, to whom it wasn't slight at all, who put their whole faith next to his, and five hundred bucks besides.

Five hundred dollars was what a family had to put down. It doesn't seem like much today. But then . . .

"My parents went every other Saturday to a meeting in New York," Yetta Ostrow tells me. "And they said to my parents they would have to pay five hundred dollars. And five hundred dollars, don't ask, was a fortune of money. At that time, in the depression, who had five hundred dollars? In New York two people had to work to pay fifty dollars a month rent. So you can imagine where they would get five hundred dollars, with eight kids. We were eight kids then. Charlie came late, he was not quite three when we moved here, he was supposed to be a six-pound tumor. And we came out to visit here several times, and my mother and father loved it. So they finally raised the five hundred dollars, and a man came down and investigated us, and we had to have papers, pictures taken of the family and everything, and it was great."

What Yetta recalls was well along in Benjamin Brown's long struggle. He had to make several false starts before he was able to reach that point. He had to cope with the well-meaning rich, with a committee of "big-shot Jews" as Myron calls them. It was hope and nothing, and again hope and nothing. It must have been hard for a man like Brown, who was full of urgency.

"He was a short, stocky man," Myron recalls, "with nice kinky hair, dark at that time. He was about forty-eight years old. He was very energetic, very intelligent. He used to walk around, quick-quick-quick, you know."

Myron is over at my house, drinking coffee, munching cake. For years, until quite recently in fact, this was a coffee-and-cake town. There was liquor in some homes—schnapps, no matter what was on the label. But cake-and-coffee is still our common lubricant of conversation; and conversation—gossip, talk, unarranged for, natural, impromptu—is still the filler for our evenings. People drive around town (now that everybody has some sort of automobile) to see whose car is at whose house and decide where they'll go accordingly. Without phoning, without invitation.

"One evening, it was in the fall of thirty-three," Myron reminisces, "I'll never forget it. Mr. Brown had a habit, after supper he would lay down on the couch and read the paper. All of a sudden he jumps up and says he's going to Washington tomorrow.

" 'Benjamin,' Sarah says, 'what are you going to do in Washington?'

" 'Look, look!' he says, all excited, 'look what it says here! President Roosevelt has formed a Homestead Division and he says he's going to build a project in every state of the Union. To decentralize industry and make all kinds of co-ops and whatnot, and I'm going to see that I get one for here.' "

"You were there, Myron?" I ask.

"I was right there in the living room," Myron asserts, and I can see the pride sticking out all over him. He's the only living witness to a historic moment. At any rate the only one in a position to talk about it around here, since Brown is dead and Mrs. Brown moved to the West Coast and since Ella, Myron's wife, had a stroke and is now in a rest home, permanently unable to contradict him.

"Mr. Brown had a friend that he knew in Utah," Myron goes on. "Mr. Broadhurst; he knew him very well because they worked together in a big poultry co-op. So the next morning he called up this Mr. Broadhurst, who was the assistant to Ickes in the Department of Interior by then, and he said 'Look, the Homestead Division the President just organized, I want you to make an appointment for me.' And he actually went to Washington that morning. That's the kind of a man he was.

"So they went to see Harold Ickes, the minister of this Department, and Mr. Ickes said: 'You'll get it, you'll get it, start buying the land.'"

"Just like that, Myron?"

"Just like that."

You may not believe him. I may not believe him. But clearly Myron believes it.

"So it didn't take more than two or three weeks, and a messenger came from Washington with a check for a hundred thousand dollars to buy the land."

"Now, wait a minute, Myron—how could the government send a check to Brown, who wasn't even connected with it, and without a survey or anything?"

Myron looks annoyed at being interrupted.

"They trusted him," he says. "They trusted him, I don't see no other way. So here's what happened with the hundred thousand: There was this Jewish farmer and he was dabbling in real estate. So they got hold of him, and they told him, here's the story, we got to buy up at least fifteen hundred acres—that was what Mr. Brown decided—and that right here would be the proper place for it.

"So this man went out one Friday afternoon—there were eleven farmers on this twelve hundred and fifty acres that we have—and he went to see all these farmers. He said: 'Look here, I think I have a customer for your farm.' And he gave them a deposit right then and there.

"In one afternoon, that Friday afternoon, he bought all the land on these farms.

"A couple of days later everybody found out that he'd bought up the whole area. So they wanted to know why they hadn't been told before, they could have jacked up the price a little bit. So this man said this was the idea, that he was buying it for a co-op, a Jewish community, and what are you complaining about, you got your money. They were ready to kill him."

What a nice, simple view of a man and an event. But then—who am I to argue with an eyewitness?

Or would you prefer something like this:

"There was a provision in the bill," Siegel explained to me, "which was not actually signed until 1933, that there would be twenty-five million dollars for subsistence projects over the entire country, and, after the local association made certain presentations, to allocate five hundred thousand dollars for this project. And they organized a federal corporation which had a daughter corporation for each project, and they established Jersey Homesteads, Inc., which was a daughter corporation of the federal corporation for this purpose."

Poor, poor Benjamin Brown.

He didn't have a chance in the world of dealing in the only way he could deal—out of his guts, out of his vision—with the do-it-through-channels men and with their (to him) contemptible willingness to wait for authorizations from on high—which really meant some office in Washington where the papers were stuck. It was a foregone conclusion that he had to break himself against the stone-hard structure as a wave must break against a sea wall.

He could be a nuisance, he could try to develop pressure by calling on Albert Einstein and Rabbi Wise and David Dubinsky. But they were busy with their own concerns, and I can well imagine that he soon wore them out. Especially Dubinsky who couldn't help suspecting an eventual runaway shop.

Brown was finished, though he didn't know it, from the moment when he prevailed on the government to underwrite the building of his dream town. Not that the paper-shufflers were necessarily corrupt or power-hungry. Quite a few of them may have started out as New Deal idealists. But to do what they were hired to do, they had to work in circumscribed ways, and after a while they couldn't help thinking in terms of budgets and requisitions rather than human beings. Brown must have been a fly buzzing past their ears. Before long, in self-preservation—no matter how much they might have respected him personally—and, of course for the good of the service, they had to get rid of him.

"The subsistence concept of daughter corporations was felt to be untenable under federal procedure," Siegel said, "and therefore the whole project was federalized. And, yes, this did put Brown out of the direction of the operation."

And so, with Brown on the outside looking in, the federalized town ground haltingly into being. On the inside were droves of employees, architects and draftsmen, surveyors and engineers, and guards, and, obviously, administrators. Several times—what with local and Congressional sniping—it looked as though the project might be abandoned. People were fired, others were hired, and the files grew in Washington. Finally the decision was made to put more money in, and a thousand workers arrived daily in buses and overloaded jalopies. And the houses started to go up.

As was to be expected, the screw-ups were innumerable. It was decided, for instance, that the houses were going to be the first prefabricated concrete dwellings, with whole walls precast in a slab plant. The scheme was ambitious: the entire side of a house was going to move through a series of buildings, with all the equipment in place, the window frames, the pipes and the electric lines, and with the concrete curing as it moved. There was only one trouble with the idea: it didn't work. The walls wouldn't stand up, they couldn't take the strain. Besides, before the procedure could be improved, an inventor turned up with a patent, a little detail nobody had taken the trouble to check. So there was nothing to do with the big slab plant except use it to produce cement blocks. These, I am told, were satisfactory. Unfortunately they cost four times as much as the same blocks bought in the open market. And so, after a while, the slab plant was dismantled. It was only a temporary structure anyway.

What Benjamin Brown felt at this time is not to be found in any writing nor any memory available to me. That he must have been hurt by his exclusion can be surmised. That he was furious is evident from his militant leadership of the prospective settlers who were waiting in New York, with their landlords on notice and their furniture about to be put on the street. Brown was their Moses, and at this stage they followed him unquestioningly— well, as unquestioningly as they could do anything. The children of Israel hadn't changed all that much since the first Moses.

The best portrait of Brown, as he must have appeared to them at that time, comes, oddly, from a youngish man who was only seven years old when he migrated with his parents out of the city into the wilderness and mud (never forget the mud) of Central New Jersey.

"To us he was like a second father," he says. "To us he looked handsome. Handsome in the way of Einstein. Larger than life. A real big doer. A Jew who could go talk to President Roosevelt. If you had a problem, you'd always think—well, Brown can solve it. He represented that marvellous mystery that got us out of that place in the Bronx. For us kids he had an almost messianic attraction. He represented the passport to our being able to play, with nobody objecting, baseball on an open field with no buildings around it."

Brown wrote letters, sent wires, chaired meetings, led delegations to Washington. How much he accomplished would be hard to tell; the paper-shufflers might have hoped to put him out to pasture, where he couldn't do much harm; but certainly he did not allow them to forget him. How much he was able to influence the selection of the settlers, I do not know. Officially the government had taken this over too.

They put in a man with the title of Senior Selection Specialist. His name was Resnick, and he had problems. The problems arose because he tried to find not only people with the appropriate skills and five hundred dollars and who were willing to take a chance on moving into the boondocks; he tried to find people who were going to be congenial. And this led to all sorts of complications.

As Edward Siegel tells it:

"Resnick got hold of a book by some professor who was making studies of this kind of thing, and soon he had us making all kinds of charts and sending out all sorts of questionnaires—if you were selected, whom would you like for your neighbor, and second-best and third-best—and we actually did try to assign houses on that basis. We had a guy on some sort of grant who started to work for us, and he made these charts and put things in different colors and moved them around till it looked like a modernistic painting. Resnick was pretty autocratic in his way of doing things, and this and the charts and the questionnaires made a lot of people pretty mad. And, of course, none of it worked out because guys who were friendly today were mortal enemies tomorrow, and if they weren't, their wives were."

I doubt very much that social science has any gauge even today to measure congeniality in neighbors; to try to foretell it is soothsaying. But then—those were innocent days when it was still possible to think of immigrant tailors becoming part-time farm workers of their own free will at farm workers' wages.

It will, I suppose, surprise nobody that Resnick was soon as generally disliked as one's neighbor who had been put there, next door, by Resnick's unforgiving, pretty chart.

Kurt Holtzman, the architect who built the town after all the earlier architects had been sent back where they came from, has a philosophical view of the matter:

"Let's go back to Schopenhauer," he says in his thick German accent. "Schopenhauer had a box and he put a bunch of porcupines in there and he watched them. And when it was very cold, they all got nicely together and that way they kept warm, you see. When it got warm, they all started sticking their quills out, and it became impossible. And this is how the human mind works."

Yet it was all so hopeful when it started: the little town only partly finished, with building still going on and people living where they could and as best they could, waiting to get into their assigned homes. And the co-op factory beginning to produce, and the co-op store in operation, and the co-op farms outside the town. It must have made Benjamin Brown feel proud, no matter what had been done to him—his idea become real, houses, factory, store and farms, and people, his people. Co-operating. As he had visualized them. If they quarreled and screamed at each other in meetings, that didn't matter, that was on the surface, and time was going to take care of it.

But it wasn't on the surface, it was deep inside these refugees from tzarism and the city who often had little in common except their Jewishness and their craft; and time didn't take care of it, time only made it worse. In spite of the Senior Selection Specialist and his questionnaires and charts, the idealist co-operators turned out to be few. A sizable portion had no intention (or capacity) to reconcile old habits with the new and very different outlook imposed by new and very different conditions of work and living. Every one of them knew how to run things better, in the town or in the factory or the store; and they weren't shy about letting everybody else know it.

There were meetings. God, how many. Every night there was

a meeting. And organizations! Insurance groups and cultural groups, national and purely local town groups and religious groups, and political groups and a lot more, where people went to make themselves heard, to complain and attack and counterattack, and occasionally to listen. I have been told that at one point the school janitor was the president of five organizations. Maybe it was democracy. It was also the symptom of a morbid condition that reached into the factory and the consumer co-op and fragmented the town.

Everybody went to the meetings. You must remember that this was before TV and that there was no way to get out—no cars to go to the movies; and no money, if there had been any. The meetings were the one amusement, open to everybody, and no tickets to pay for. And the show was worth watching.

"I used to love to go to the meetings," Stella remembers. "It was like going to the theatre. I loved the beautiful flow of Yiddish. I used to speak to these same people on the street in English, and it was painful, their English was so stilted. But when they got up on the floor and spoke in Yiddish, they assumed a more manly, a more powerful stature, they became beautifully oratorical. Later on, when there began to be a few English-speaking people, somebody from the floor would yell: 'Talk English! Talk English!' and people would insist on talking in Yiddish, and then, before the meeting could start, there would be this big floor fight about talk Yiddish, talk English. There were always fierce disagreements that came out at these meetings, about anything at all, any triviality. These were poor people who had to work with each other every day in a very structured situation that was really foreign to them. And often they had a very low regard for each other, and by the time they came to the meeting, all their self-hatred and hatred for the others came out. They were always afraid the other guy was trying to get an edge on them."

It didn't take very long for the resentments and suspicions to spill over on the economic organisms that were basic to the community as Benjamin Brown had conceived it. They weren't being run right, somebody else was getting more money, the manager was a no-good. Sometimes, even now, thirty years later, an injustice still rankles.

25

Yetta Ostrow is a pale, sharp-faced, middle-aged woman, a member of one of several clans which at some point or another were powerful in town. Her brother Barry was the big man in the right wing of local politics during later years. After the father died, Barry ran the clan; he was its leading member, under the uncompromising guidance of his mother who used to be a public voice in her own right. (Now she's a wraith of an old lady, bent over and gnarled, with red-rimmed suspicious eyes—tragic as age is tragic when coupled with infirmity—and devoted to a black miniature poodle.) Yetta is in her mother's image: sickly but resistant, painfully thin, bitter of tongue, and a powerful hater beneath her pile of red hair. When I listen to her talk, I get the notion that she is angry at her brother Barry for dying prematurely and thus depriving her of reflected glory.

"We really loved this place," she says. "When my father came, he was made foreman in the cloak factory, and it caused a lot of friction and jealousy because one made two cents more than the other one. If somebody found out that you made a penny more an hour than the next guy—after all, you were doing a bigger job than the next guy—literally they knifed you in the back. I mean with words. Some of them would knife you in the back and spit in your face. One of the men that spit in my mother's face is still here. She was one of the designers, and she told him he was doing something wrong, and he said to her: 'No woman is going to tell me what's right and what's wrong.' And he spit in her face, honey. My father—may he rest in peace—couldn't accept it when the people refused to take orders, and he quit."

I can believe her. She doesn't accept it easily either when people refuse to take her orders.

"I believe in living this way," she says. "It goes down perfect. Why should it happen in a small community like this? . . . We had a tearoom in a corner of the store that was fabulous. Everybody went to the tearoom, kids, grownups, everybody. We had ice cream and sundaes, whatever you wanted, tea, coffee, anything. And we had Walter Winchell that worked there. She was Maxine Solomon who's now Maxine Diamond. If you wanted to know anything about what was going on in town, honey, Walter Winchell told you. And the greatest Brooklyn accent in the world. Now she's a great lady and she's become British. Excuse me. But then she was plain Maxine Solomon. . . . And the store—it was nothing but a shack, but it was a pleasure to walk into because everyone was so warm. The fruit was there, old-fashioned, the box of oranges and the box of lettuce and Mr. Buxbaum. At that time we used to go to the store and pluck our own chickens. So help me God. You can ask any woman that lived here at the time. It was such a warm feeling, this one plucking hers and that one blowing on another to see if the chicken had a little more fat. And we had a butcher, and Buxbaum cut fish. He was a marvellous grocer and fish man. It was fabulous."

But it wasn't as idyllic as it looks to Yetta in retrospect. At the store, as at the factory, hostilities crept in; as often as they could get a lift, people would go into Hightstown to shop, and after a while they sold their shares. And a lot of the anger turned against Brown, the originator, who by then was desperately trying to hold his co-operatives together.

But there was trouble at the factory, too. Orders were delivered late; rejects were frequent. Cohesion and direction were lost, confusion brought more resentment, and workmanship suffered. There were strikes—short-lived but still strikes. You wouldn't think people would strike against themselves. But they did.

For an example, let Goldie tell it:

"One day the machine broke, and they couldn't finish out the work, so my husband told them: 'You know what, let Goldie come in and make the bottoms.' Because I was a finisher. So I went in for a day. So they all stopped working, all the men, and they made a strike. Because one woman came in the shop. So Benjamin Brown found out what's going on, so he said: 'If this goes on like this, take all the women what knows how to work, take them into the shop and throw out the men.' That's what he told them. They didn't like it and they didn't do it. They were on strike for four days. Then they went back, and I stayed because they needed me to put on the buttons and make the hems and everything."

There was trouble on the farms as well. Some of it was pretty funny, some of it was sad. All of it must have added up to a terrible disturbance in the mind and soul of Benjamin Brown.

Bernarda Shahn tells a story about what happened at the dairy barn—a story which illustrates, I think, how things were falling apart.

"I can tell you how the dairy farm came a cropper," she says. "It wasn't working; things were not going at all well. Deliveries were getting more and more unperiodic. There were complaints. Finally an expert was called in, a professional milk chemist and dairyman. He was a Frenchman, and it was a great coincidence that Ben had happened to know him when he was in France. And after his inspection this man came over to our house for dinner, and he and Ben were delighted to see each other. And then he started to laugh, and he told us what he had been called for and what his adventures had been.

"It seems that he found the barn in foul condition. The cows were standing waist-deep in their own offal. So Jacques (that was his name) found that the manure conveyor had stopped working, and he said to them: 'Let's have a look at it, we'll probably have to call in somebody to put it in condition.' But when he went out in back, there was a mountain of manure. The conveyor was dead stuck in the mountain of manure. It couldn't have moved. And Jacques asked them: 'For God's sake, how did you let this manure pile up this way? Don't you carry it away once a week?'

"They told him that the rick in which it was carried away had disappeared. Somebody had stolen it.

"So Jacques told them to, for God's sake, shovel it away. And they got some people with shovels and they began shoveling and they found the rick under the mountain of manure. And they got the dairy working again. For a while anyway."

It is, I think, interesting, that nobody else I talked to admits knowing anything about this story. Maybe they honestly don't know; maybe they don't want to know, it's too embarrassing even at this distance.

There are dozens of other stories, and all of them pathetic. Certainly none of them were funny to Benjamin Brown, because in the long run they killed him.

Not the stories, but the strife and deterioration they represented. A deterioration in work and spirit which was always blamed on Brown, as it had to be, inevitably, since he was the father of it all. And so finally the unspeakable happened, and Benjamin Brown was voted off the board of the co-operative.

He didn't live long after that, I am told. The tales differ: some say that he disappeared and wasn't found until several days later wandering through the streets of New York City, not knowing who or where he was. Others tell of him being picked up walking aimlessly in the Holland Tunnel. It doesn't matter. The spirit of a minor prophet was smashed by his creation, his temple falling on him, as the temple had fallen down on Samson.

He lived for a while after his breakdown, and then died, no doubt of some prosaic and ordinary disease, like the stopping of the heart.

4

There must be hundreds of studies of new settlements and how they grow. Especially in these days, when artificially created communities become more common all the time. The day of the planner is upon us—the environmental planner, the industrial planner, the professional houser. And the natural, organic growth of hamlets into villages into towns and finally into cities (around a grist mill on a creek, at a crossroads or a rail junction or on the shore of a ready-made harbor) has become impractical. It takes too long. It's too chaotic, too wasteful. And so, within a wastefulness far greater than any conceivable before, we plan neat units within the big, spreading cancer: a housing project, the latest thing in real estate developments. As though it were possible to isolate them from the national disaster; as though it were possible to predict precisely what, in the long run, is going to happen in any agglomeration of human beings—in a country where the majority moves every few years and in a world where the balance between existence and nonexistence is so precarious that nobody can look at it for long.

Our town can serve as warning. Because here nothing developed as planned: the community found its own form and feeling, perversely, you might say, to become something nobody could possibly have foreseen.

The process started early, well before Brown's death. The

shortage of houses changed to a surplus. The Senior Selection Specialist found fewer and fewer candidates who fitted the original prescription: even people who had signed up earlier now backed out. There were rumors that the factory was in trouble and that living in the project had its drawbacks; and five hundred dollars was as hard to raise as ever. For a long time nearly a hundred houses stood empty.

Nearby Millstone Township refused to accept the children from the suspect community in its schools. That it was Jewish was bad enough; that it was reputed to be Red was worse. It had to fail. No doubt about it. The government wasn't going to nursemaid it forever. And then who was going to pay for running those newfangled luxuries, like a water treatment plant and a complete sewage system for two hundred houses no respectable person would consider living in? Not the farmers, you bet. Not around here, where all the farm leaders were Republican and proud of their conservatism.

So, while it was still a government project, Jersey Homesteads had to take on the load of its own grade school, to be financed, theoretically, from property taxes nobody had the money to pay.

It was frightening:

1 teaching principal	$1,800 a year
5 elementary school teachers . . .	$6,500 a year
1 janitor	$1,300 a year

The government was going to have to help out. What else could it do?

The government showed forbearance. Not only did it cover the delinquent payments in lieu of taxes, it even made a substantial loan to the co-op factory when it lost money during its first year. But when the budget kept climbing, and no decrease in sight, the administration acted. It put the empty houses up for rent. To anybody, Jewish or non-Jewish, regardless of skill or profession or any other category, as long as his income was low enough.

A simple action. A reasonable action; you could easily consider it a minor one.

32

It split the community into two halves. Now the warriors had a secondary target: the government remaining, of course, number one. The homesteaders, with their unforgotten and unforgiven five hundred dollars as a club, turned on the newcomers. How dare they speak up at meetings? They hadn't paid the price of admission. They hadn't lived through the hard times before the streets were paved, when it was worth your life to cross from corner to corner in the mud. The five hundred dollars and the mud: these were the symbols of hardship endured, of merit acquired. And here, suddenly, were two classes in this tiny town where nobody had any money to speak of: on one side the homesteaders, the Plymouth Rock people, the Mayflower people; on the other side the renters, the tenants.

"We moved in about that time," Jules Goldblatt says. "We were still living with another family, waiting to get into a house of our own. And I went to one of those meetings. There was a very heated discussion, and I got up to put in my two cents, and this old homesteader—who had paid his five hundred dollars—got up, with his neck getting scarlet and said: 'Look who's talking! Not a homesteader, not a tenner*—a boarder by a tenner!'

"It brought down the house. Everyone started yelling: 'Let him talk, let him talk!'

"And the homesteaders got up on their chairs and started yelling: 'Shut up, he can't talk! He can't talk!'

"I talked all right. I doubt that I was heard. And I don't remember now what it was all about."

Jules was no garment worker. He was younger than most, a college man, I believe, with a lovely delicate wife and two children. Later on he got the job of town engineer, in charge of water supply and sewage. Jules fitted in: he had as sharp a tongue as anyone, homesteader or renter. And he usually got what he wanted.

Once, after he'd been living in town for some time, he heard that a desirable house was going to be vacated—a bigger and better house than he was then occupying—and he decided to get it.

"I went to Ed Siegel, the administrator and my boss, and I

* a tenant

put in a bid for the house," Jules explains. "And then Mrs. Pinkus, Yetta's mother, went to him a couple of days later, and she says: 'I want this house for Yetta.'

"So Siegel says: 'Well, she has only one child.'

"She said: 'She's going to have more, she's pregnant.'

"He said: 'Jules Goldblatt put in a bid before you.'

"She said: 'That's nothing. I've lived here longer. He's just a renter.'

"She was one of those people who had walked in the mud of the town, and Belle and I were just newcomers. It took a long time before we got over that second-class feeling. . . .

"So Siegel said: 'I don't know what to say.' He didn't want to give the impression that he was favoring one of his employees. But, since we had asked first and we did have two kids . . .

"I told him: 'I'm no slouch either. I'll make Belle pregnant too.' At least that's what I told him.

"So Siegel said: 'All right, we'll put both names into a hat and we'll pull one.'

"She said: 'Let the rabbi do it.' She knew the rabbi was on her side because she was the president of the shul or something.

"So the poor rabbi comes around and he puts both names into his hat, and he asks her: 'Should I draw one?'

"So she said: 'Yes,' and so he drew one and she said: 'What is it?' And with fear and trembling he said it was Goldblatt.

"She looked at him—you know how she can look at people even now—and she says: 'I always knew you weren't much of a rabbi.'

"Soon after that the rabbi left town. But we got the house."

And the town filled up. Most of the new renters were still Jewish, although there are several Italian and Irish-Catholic families who came in at that time and who are still here, they or their children. I can well imagine that in their beginnings in this Jewish town they must have felt as cut off and surrounded as any Jew in a Gentile suburb.

It was during that period that Ben Shahn rented a house. He was already known. Everybody had gone to watch him paint his big mural in the school the year before. They couldn't quite figure out what to make of him up there on his scaffold, doing things they couldn't understand. But they were proud that their school was going to have this big, big picture in it.

But the artist? Well, they had never known a "paintner" before. They weren't particularly impressed. They supposed that painting pictures was a craft, as cloak-making was a craft, and they didn't think there was anything so special about it. He was a Jewish man, and that helped, even if he did have a goyish wife. It's my personal opinion—with which a number of mutual friends disagree—that Jewish culture is the Word, not the image (probably because of the Biblical prohibition against making graven images) and that therefore there was, in this enclave, no precedent for thinking of an image-maker in the same light as a scholar or a doctor or a lawyer. Ben spoke to them in their vernacular, and that was nice; occasionally he showed a totally unexpected acquaintance with the complex minutiae of customs and scripture, and that astonished them.

Lou and Sara Perlmutter tell a story:

"He was painting the mural at the time," Lou told me. "And it was interesting to see an artist work, we all would go over and watch, and he didn't mind. And we were thrilled because this whole thing was ours. The school was ours, the walls, everything. And this beautiful picture was going to be ours. We were thrilled even if we had no interest in painting at all. But it's the nights that I remember, when Ben would leave Bernarda home with Suzy—Johnny wasn't born yet—and come over to the house. I can remember him sitting in that chair till two in the morning. One particular night, we had more people, and he was describing visiting an island off the north shore of Africa, and he described how he got there on the Sabbath eve, and some Jews gave him food to eat, and he couldn't make out what it was and then he discovered that it was locusts.

"And Sasha Graditz, who was very well versed in religion, said: 'Oh, that can't be, this is not kosher.' Sasha was a real orthodox.

"And Ben says: 'The hell it can't. If you'll turn to the book . . .' And he knew the page and all, eh.

"And Abe Aschkenazi was sitting there—his mother is more orthodox than the rabbi—and he went home to get the book, eh.

35

The old lady nearly got sick because of the thought that this bug was kosher. In the meantime Ben bet Sasha that whoever was wrong was going to have to eat a locust, a grasshopper. But, eh, you know, Ben knew the page and the paragraph, just where to find it in the book. And when Abe came back, there it was."

I don't believe that Sasha Graditz had to eat a grasshopper. But, of course the story spread, and everybody laughed. At the same time people were a little impressed with the knowledge of scripture evidently possessed by this big bear of a friendly man with his round, close-cropped, Germanic-looking head and the peculiar passion to lock himself up every day to dab paint on pictures that didn't sell. And there were other similar stories, and Ben was gradually accepted even by the homesteaders—though probably with some reserve—as another member of the community. If he had his eccentricities, well, the world was full of odd people.

It was different with Brown and Holtzman, the architect. They had traveled, they had a worldly education. They could recognize the potential of this struggling painter whose importance to his period was still only known to a few museum directors and avant-garde collectors. They could see that Ben was literate in many areas, from social movements to science to psychology and history; there wasn't a novel or a sit-down strike on which he didn't have strong and usually controversial opinions.

How he saw himself in relation to the town and its people probably wasn't clear even to himself at this early stage. Bernarda tells me that, when they first settled here, they had no thought of staying more than a year or two. It wouldn't have occurred to either of them that they might end up keeping the same house all those long years until Ben's death in 1968.

And it wouldn't have occurred even to Brown and Holtzman that the day was going to come when the presence of this brilliant oddball was going to be as important in forming the reputation and character of the town as the presence of Benjamin Brown had been in founding it.

Some time before he died Brown dreamed up a project that brought him and Ben and Holtzman into a brief collaboration. He tried to start a labor college on his land. Labor was the hero then, remember: the workingman was going to solve the problems that frustrated everyone else. There was going to be a library containing all obtainable material directly or indirectly connected with labor, theoretically, historically, legally, idealistically, fiction and fact. And around his library a school was going to function, the only labor-oriented college in a country where higher education was almost universally classics-oriented. And to discuss his plan, he drew in a number of people who might have ideas to contribute, among them Kurt Holtzman and Ben Shahn. They were going to call it Veblen College. At a preliminary meeting with some dissident professors (being prolabor was practically subversive then), Holtzman was asked to develop a physical design and Ben was commissioned to conceive a visual arts training center.

They both did their jobs. Holtzman built a complete model based on the contour of Brown's land and including buildings, facilities, everything. Ben worked out a plan for apprenticeship training in presswork and graphics of all sorts from posters to college publications, from books to labels. Everything was great. Everything was hopeful.

What happened at the second meeting, the important one that was to start the project toward reality, I'll let Bernarda tell:

"The two weeks of the conference came around," she says, "and there were people from everywhere: writers, professors, labor people, somebody from *The Nation,* and I think a couple of poets. People sat on benches and on chairs and on the ground under the trees and food was served and everybody was housed in the big old house that is still there. Lots of people came during some of the sessions. Einstein came with his sister. And then the professors began quarreling among themselves, and nobody would accept anybody else's plan. It was a shambles.

"It was obvious before long that nothing was going to come of the conference. These people were simply not qualified to get along with each other. We soon recognized that there was very little dedication among them, that they had come to the conference only because each one was dreaming of a cushy little nest in which to spend the last years of his life agreeably."

Was this so strange? Could it be that all of Benjamin

Brown's projects suffered from this same miscalculation? That he counted on everyone for an unselfishness equal to his own? Or was it passion? An uncommon form of selfishness akin to the artist's drive? Perhaps.

Probably he was lucky to die in time. So that he did not have to watch his dream factory disintegrate—that indispensable link in the chain of modest but important institutions essential to make his model community what he had willed it to be.

Why did the factory fail? Take your choice of causes: amateurish management, high costs, poor workmanship, sloppy deliveries, strikes and fights, covert opposition by the national union. It could be said that they all contributed. And when the government finally refused to pull the little factory out of the hole again, there was nothing for it, they had to fold. And for a bitter interval the once so hopeful tailors had to settle for laying curbs and digging ditches. Which was not what they had come out to the country to do.

And so some of the most vigorous of the homesteaders found jobs outside of town, in Trenton and Asbury Park and Freehold and as far away as Philadelphia. It took time to find the jobs, and it was a terrible disappointment: what had they paid their money for, if not assured employment for the rest of their lives? But most of them were far too obstinate to capitulate to mere misfortune. They were well acquainted with bad luck: they had been on familiar terms with it since they were born. Only a few moved out of town. The rest got along somehow. They hitched, they jammed themselves into jalopies that shouldn't have been allowed on the road; some accepted retraining as hat-makers when a private company rented the building they had thought of as their own. And of course they grumbled.

The co-op store lasted a while longer. People remember it with affection. They smile when they talk about it.

"This was in the days before adding machines," Belle Goldblatt recalls, "and you got your bill added up on a paper bag, with a pencil that was licked. And Mr. Levi—he was the number-two man—was a little bit hard of hearing. So you'd ask, for example, for margarine, and he'd give you marshmallows. And you didn't want to hurt his feelings, so you took the marshmallows. And he'd do all this in a most leisurely fashion, and it was almost lunch time and the kids would be coming home and there would be a line of ladies waiting. But he took his time. He would lick his pencil before every number and then he'd add out loud."

Not Mr. Buxbaum. He was the boss grocer, and he prided himself on doing all the adding in his head, and he claimed that he never made a mistake. And nobody dared question him about it because he had a capacity for insult second to none. He was the only man in town who had two picket lines to look back on, one against him, the other in his favor. Milton Stein refers to him as the man who survived Jewish women.

"Buxbaum had been hardened by years of Jewish women," Milton says. "He buried one and he was in the future to survive several more. To him a Jewish lady shopper was a challenge and he could handle them. He would stand back and watch them come in, and he would wait for them to make one slip, and he would decimate them. They would leave the store in tears."

There is no resentment left, even among the ladies he treated with such classic rudeness. But then there was general and growing anger. People were patient for a while, and then they called a meeting and threw a picket line around the store. Somebody told me—I don't remember who it was—that the ladies on the picket line carried signs saying: "Buxbaum must go."

The meeting must have been phenomenal. Everybody turned out. There was standing room only. And the discussion raged around the question of Buxbaum's insufferable behavior and whether it was right to fire him. The accused sat quietly and listened to the arguments, until he thought the moment was ripe. Then he asked for the floor.

"It was the climax of the evening," Belle says. "A hush fell over the house, and he got up, and such a Ciceronian oration I have never heard. He spoke of himself in the third person, in perfectly balanced arguments. It was Shakespearean. He went on and on, and everyone was sitting there open-mouthed, in admiration of his ability to orate. In the end he received a big round of applause. He was a great actor."

You would never have thought so to look at him. He was tall and skinny and bald, with an insignificant bad-boy's face usually screwed up in an expression of distaste. He did know his business. About this there is no disagreement. He was an excellent grocer.

There is one more story about him, which may not be factual. I include it, because, in my opinion it sums him up.

While the attack on him was mounting daily, he is supposed to have said to a flock of screaming women that, if they were going to hang him anyway, would they please hang him with his face to the wall.

"Why?" somebody asked.

"So's you can all kiss my ass."

Maybe it's true, maybe it isn't. My hat is off to the fighting grocer who either spoke those words or inspired them.

Buxbaum wasn't fired. He stayed on even after the co-op disintegrated to run the town store under private ownership. Years later he left, an old man, as most good homesteaders seem to leave, for Florida.

The co-op store failed for lack of support and because of internal disagreements. It died also, I suspect, of the automobile.

There were beginning to be a few more cars in town. People no longer depended entirely on the local store; shopping out of town, now that it was easier, was certainly more glamorous. And this was the start of a far-reaching change which eventually was to make the community over into something nobody then had a name for. It brought the world in; over the years it blurred the sharp outlines of separation. And the town, to the extent it could, started to join New Jersey.

5

You might say that the architect and the occupants soon to come coexisted on widely separated floors of their many-layered time.

The architect, not long out of Germany, still spoke in what amounted to a burlesque of a German accent. His ideas had been formed at the Bauhaus. He considered himself an urbanist and he must have known about Letchworth and Welwyn Gardens. Judging by the spare functionalism of his design for the Homesteads, I would suspect that his (then) avant-garde taste was influenced by the sophisticated rectilinear purity of Le Corbusier.

The immigrant tailors had very different expectations. They were looking forward to their own dream of the rural life: cozy cottages, perhaps with scrolled woodwork gingerbread around gabled roofs, and with primroses climbing up clapboard walls flanked by green shutters that could be closed and locked.

When the families arrived to take possession, they were rendered acutely uncomfortable by the concrete boxes with their floor-to-ceiling windows and their flat roofs pressing down on rooms that seemed to them unduly cramped compared to their vision of Utopia.

A few tried bricking up portions of the big glass areas that looked out on what must have been a pretty desolate, almost tree-less landscape. They were soon disabused. Any alterations, even

41

the most insignificant, had to be approved by the project manager, and such approval was not easy to obtain: if you wanted your kitchen painted, it must be green, government green, the stockpiled kitchen color and no other. And so they had to be satisfied with flossy curtains, since they were concerned far more with keeping the outside from looking in than with looking out. It must have taken an act of will to try to like the houses and to admit that, maybe, the concrete boxes weren't so ugly after all.

It was really a lot to ask of them: that they should fit themselves into the bare and undecorated functionalism that was modern at the time. It was, in fact, the imposition of one culture on another, a minor rape of minds, to demand of them that they make themselves over in an image that was in no way their own. Because, as immigrants—early refugees, if you like—they had at least one wrench behind them: from Poland or Russia to Brooklyn or the Bronx, from the *stetl* to the great, the incomprehensible, the American city. They had made this step, at a cost varying with individuals. And each in his own way had learned to visualize the Promised Land (which this country was to them) in a composite of the ideal derived from the illustrations in the *Saturday Evening Post*.

Not that many of them read the *Post*. Most had got their view of the existing American world from the pushcart-lined streets outside of the tenements and from the Yiddish columns of the *Forward* or the *Freiheit*. But their aspirations must have been partly formed by their children who brought home from school and from the public library a jigsaw puzzle shaped from the pastorals in books and current magazines. As usual, the children were the first to be subjected to the adventure and wrath of a change their parents were not yet ready to accept.

It started here at the very beginning. Bill Perlmutter and Herman Rosenzweig remember what it was like:

"When we came to Allentown before our own school was finished, less than forty of us into a school of about four hundred —here came the Jew bus. In Allentown they were farm kids and they knew about Jews, but they never knew that they came in such numbers and in such various shapes. New York Jewish kids who didn't know an apple from a cow.

42

"We soon found out that the farmers didn't know how to fight. They were much stronger and you wouldn't let them get their hands on you, but they couldn't stand up and square off and do an adequate job. Kids in this area—it was a lot of talk and pushing. The New York kids were tougher, they had much more experience. But even so . . .

"The problem went right on through high school because the bus from the Homesteads with its Jewish kids kept coming and coming. And they were waiting for us. And you always had one or two on the bus who you weren't particularly proud of. Like, we had a little fat one who looked real Jewish, and you would have liked him to disappear into the woodwork. But he was yours, and there wasn't a hell of a lot you could do about it. Or you'd have one with a lot of mouth, who was something you wouldn't want to hang a tag on and say: 'He comes to school with me.' But in that farmers' school we stuck together and fought together."

"When I went to Allentown High School," Herman adds, "I was a tough little bastard. I was the one they used to have to fight out in front of the bus, so that they could get at the rest of our kids. I used to have to fight maybe three or four times a week. I think that the kids who grew up here and had to go through this kind of fighting, realized that any minority group is in danger of being annihilated by the majority. I had to fight a Negro only once, because he wanted to identify himself with the white guys, and by doing that, you know, if you beat up a Jew, you were in business. I beat him, but it was a terrible fight for me. Although I was only fourteen years old, I somehow realized what his motivation was, and I swore I would never do it again.

"The older people in town had this schizophrenia too. On the one hand they distrusted goyim, it was built into them. On the other hand there were certain goyim who were in the same shoes they were in themselves. And so this antigoyishness started to break down with the second generation. Naturally you didn't get over it all the way overnight.

"I remember coming home from Philadelphia—I was already grown up—just to show you how this thing can hang on over all these years—and there was a very heavy snowstorm. The kind that chokes the road. And I wanted to get home before the town was completely blocked off. And I got stuck in a drift.

"I sat there in the car, and the snow was really coming down and blowing, and I couldn't get out for more than an hour and I started to freeze.

"Suddenly at my window there were these two black faces. And my first impulse was to roll up the window and just sit there, ready for anything, until, hopefully, they went away. But, you know why they stopped? They stopped to push me out of the drift I was in.

"And I drove home with this enormous sense of guilt: that out in this cold, black night, when these two guys showed up, my first impulse was to defend myself. . . ."

On first meeting you might not think of Herman as a man of conscience. He's tall and very erect and he wears a small, well-barbered goatee. He's concerned with his presence, you can tell that, a result, no doubt, of many performances in opera houses from San Francisco to Naples, Italy. He discovered that he had a voice almost by accident, while he was in the Army and found himself singing with the U.S. Army band. Since then he's enjoyed his work, I'm sure, even the cocktail parties in second-rate towns he claims to despise. The going has been rough for him and his family. I guess he worries sometimes, because, unless he makes it big, how long can a man remain a competent, better than average opera singer?

The people in town accept him, of course. But they don't yet accord him the special respect they gave his father, the idealistic tailor. If he makes it as a star—maybe. Or if he had become a famous cantor . . .

Herman has remodeled his house extensively. He put in a lot of money, probably more than he could afford. Lately he had a chance to sell it. At the last minute he couldn't.

"This is my town," he says. "If anybody wants to reach me, even on the road, all they have to write on the envelope is: Herman, Roosevelt, New Jersey.

*

44

Depressions tend to be periods of innovation. The standard remedies don't work—all right, let's try something new.

The miserable thirties produced a certain amount of human caring for human beings—there was just enough threat in the air for that—and for the first time in American history artists were included. Confronted with the evident failure of the perfect economic system, America was ashamed, and the normal American feeling of cultural inferiority became obsessive. If Europe was full of murals, dammit, why shouldn't we be? All over the country post offices and other similarly astonished public buildings were having their murals painted.

There was not only an artists' union; there were federal art projects.

It would be hard to imagine a building less likely to receive an impressive mural than the school in this out-of-the-way community with nothing around it except a lot of agriculture. It got one. And Ben Shahn was brought in to paint it.

It turned out to be a very large mural, even as murals go, running the length of the school lobby, above a brick wall. It teems with people. Immigrants arrive at Ellis Island and walk ashore, led by Albert Einstein, past two coffins containing the dead Sacco and Vanzetti; toward the center tailors work at their machines and a workers' school beckons. The pivotal figure is a chesty, oversize labor leader making a speech above a crowd of faces and beneath the building where the Triangle Fire trapped almost a hundred and fifty women machine operators. The labor leader looks just like a pompous John L. Lewis (though Ben always insisted that the figure isn't meant to resemble anyone in particular). After a transition from this thunderous crescendo, a group of planners plan: the new community grows under their hands. They include portraits of such worthies of the time as Heywood Broun and David Hillman who really had little if anything to do with Jersey Homesteads.

The mural remains. A generation of schoolchildren has gone from kindergarten through the eighth grade under its ponderous simplifications. Any number of affairs, from PTA meetings to lectures and cake sales, have taken place below this monument to

45

momentous actions and issues that have become less momentous with the years. Somehow, except in a few passages, it is too specific to wear time well. It seems to me that, unlike so much of Ben's work, it fails to reach out from its period; and what may have been dramatic when it was painted, now is little more than a slogan in a language that is no longer completely understood. Yet the mural, like the houses themselves, must have had its effect on the homesteaders in their new, demanding environment. And certainly on their children.

Although sometimes I wonder. One of the kids, when asked to describe the mural he passed daily on his way to the gym, is supposed to have said: "They came to America and they worked on sewing machines, and then they all became architects."

*

Stella speaking:

"By the time Ben moved here, he was, in his relationship to the community, like an expatriate living in a colorful country. But at the same time it was also his country. And so, sometimes he'd get annoyed with its failings because they were very close failings. He was both in and out of it.

"Ben made a mistake, I think, about people here at that time, in that he felt a lack of respect for what was closest to them. Now, people don't really mind a lack of respect toward your individual self, but a lack of respect toward your cultural self is intolerable.

"There was that time when there was a professor who taught agriculture at Rutgers and who used to come to this town. And this man gave a speech and said something about really the Jews were the greatest and the most intelligent people in the world. Now, that didn't strike any Jew in the audience as a racist remark at all, any more than it strikes Negroes when one of them gets up and says they are so great. They took it as an accolade to their cultural selves. To exist as Jews for five thousand beleaguered years—they had to believe, by God, that they were worth it.

"But Ben got furious. He yelled out something. He denounced the man. It was a very bitter thing. And he got angry at the people who were there. . . . He knew that they could be better than that, and he wished them to transcend their smallness and fulfill the Godly promise. He wanted his people to be MAN in the Biblical sense, and he was upset by their human pettiness.

"That was in him then, and it set up a lot of tensions because he was always getting angry at them for being smaller than they ought to be. At the same time he liked their smallness because it was familiar and human. It was very complex. On the one hand he would delight in conversations with the school janitor, and this one and that one. On the other hand he could be furious with him for listening to this Rutgers professor proclaiming that We the Jews are the greatest and believing it. Because this was the smallness side of it. . . ."

*

By the time Ben settled here after the houses were thrown open to anybody, this provincial village offered not nearly enough to nourish him. He was forever going out of town for long periods, painting murals elsewhere, or, with his Leica equipped with angle finder, studying the lives of unimportant people in places that were not getting much concerned attention: places like Kentucky and Arkansas and the towns and cotton fields of Mississippi.

Here in town he couldn't keep his hands off. He had to get involved. He was an involved kind of man. Direct and personal involvement was at the root of what he was and what he painted. There was anger in many of the images that poured out of him then, in his prime. At least it looked like anger. Actually, I suspect that a passion for justice was at the bottom of everything he did. Justice, which is a much deeper thing than the American concept of fairness, since this is based, after all, on the good-natured observance of the rules of games. It is entirely possible that his vision of a just world had been implanted by his father and grandfather in the tough kid who devoured books in the public library and did his first fighting in the streets of Brooklyn, New York.

The trouble was, of course, that in a small place any convinced believer in the perfectibility of man had to become a pest. With his scale of sins against the spirit, he was equipped to measure and attack intolerance and meanness with the same furious energy nationally or in the town. Inevitably he antagonized more than he persuaded.

He fought successfully against a *yeshivah* in the public school, and on this issue he had allies among the old-line socialists. But how many of the yiddishists could understand that this contentious champion popping up suddenly out of nowhere was defending the separation of church and state? Separation, schmetteration! He had a goyish wife.

In a campaign against a heavy-handed mayor, Ben and Bernarda and some of their newfangled friends sent out a leaflet entitled: WHO RUNS JERSEY HOMESTEADS? And in the body of the leaflet they answered their own question: A TAMMANY CLIQUE RUNS JERSEY HOMESTEADS. Well . . .

Tammany then, much more than now, was the generic name for reaction, double-dealing, Christmas turkey politicking and Boss Tweed, who was still remembered. How could anybody so insult the neighbor he gossipped with in yiddish, whom he called by his first name when he met him on the street? Small-town politics differs from big-city politics chiefly because the contenders are in the round rather than flat and gray and paper-thin. In a small town you know what ails each one of them because you have heard him tell about it. In person. He may have strong opinions, and they may differ from your own, and the chances are that he didn't arrive at them any more rationally than you did. But each has an investment in his own goodness in which he must believe: a tremulous faith he safeguards with all his guile and all his mustered anger, lest his core be injured and life become insupportable. And it was this vital belief that was threatened by Ben's leaflet. People were outraged. Damned if they were going to be put in the same pot with crooks and the Oppressors of The People.

The rancor stayed. On both sides, after its cause had long receded. Under all the pleasant talk and the coffee and cake and the many expressions of mutual affection and esteem.

*

Murray Greenbaum would go broke if he didn't let his better credit risks sign slips for what they buy at the modest but neon-lighted and air-conditioned store he built some years ago after the old one burned down. He would lose even more of his business to the Acme and the A & P and the Shop-Rite that have proliferated in Hightstown since the publishing company and the RCA Space Center and a lot of smaller industries have brought thousands of new people to the area.

It's a shame to see the worry lines creep over Murray's thin, anxious face. Murray is the sort of man who is referred to as un-failingly courteous. Only very seldom does he lose his temper with some woman who gives him a hard time over a loaf of Jewish rye, which is all she ever comes in for. That, and maybe a pack of Newports or Pall Malls late on a Saturday evening.

Murray didn't come here to be a grocer. More than thirty years ago, after Brown's dream factory died, he arrived in town as manager of a privately owned hat factory which was being set up in the empty building. He was a bringer of hope then, tall and young and sandy-haired, friendly and full of confidence. He knew that there were plenty of skilled people who needed work. The fact that their skill was of a different order didn't bother him. They were used to machines and to doing complicated things with their hands: they were going to be easy to retrain.

They learned fast, he was right about that. Most of them any-way. His problems as factory manager proved to be of different dimension.

"There was Mr. and Mrs. Lebowitz, for instance," Murray says. "She worked in the shipping department and he worked as an operator. They were both around fifty-five years old.

"One day he walks into my office with a valise.

"'What's the matter, Mr. Lebowitz?' I need a guy to leave a machine empty like a hole in the head.

"'I'm going away. I can't bear my wife. I can't bear my house. She's driving me crazy. If I stand, she wants me to sit. If I sit, she wants me to stand. If I read the paper, she says what are you reading for? She's driving me nuts.'

"It was known that this was true. As a matter of fact, one day she drove him to such distraction, he ran out of the house naked."

"I said to him: 'Mr. Lebowitz, you're a grandfather. How can a man of your age leave his wife? People are going to say that either you were caught with somebody or your wife was caught with somebody.'

"I said: 'Do me a favor. Go sit down at your machine and let me talk to your wife. . . .'

"So I called the wife to my office and she sat down, and I told my secretary to take a walk.

"'Mrs. Lebowitz,' I said, 'did you know that your husband came in with a valise today and that he is ready to leave you?'

"She said: 'What can I do? He's crazy, he's this, he's that.'

"So I told her the same thing, that people were going to say it was unfaithfulness on his or her part.

"She said: 'What can I do? What can I do?'

"I said to her: 'Will you listen to me? When he comes home tonight, give him supper and make believe he's not there. If he sits, let him sit. If he reads the paper, let him read.'

"And I walked over to Mr. Lebowitz at his machine, and I said to him: 'Mr. Lebowitz, try it for another week. I think it will be all right.'

"He took his valise home. He came to work. Everything is fine. Two days later Mrs. Lebowitz walks in with a package and drops it on my desk. And I open it up, and it's a cake.

"'What's this?' I say to her.

"'Darling,' she says to me, 'you gave me back my husband.'

"There were many incidents like that, believe me. But I had a feeling for these people. I came from the same background. I understood them."

Did he now? What Murray called understanding—a general sharing of common experience—may have been good enough, as far as it went. But since he was a newcomer then, and a straw boss at that, he wasn't prepared to include the dream, he couldn't be specific and local enough in his understanding. Not that it would have helped much if he had understood, I suppose. The dream was there, left over like furniture from an occupant who had passed away, and what was anybody going to do with it?

Benjamin Brown's dream, the dream the homesteaders had

been so hot about because of what it offered, and sometimes so lukewarm, because of what it demanded.

It was their factory, wasn't it? The fact that a New York exploiter had rented it from the government to make money (and incidentally hats) was his problem, not theirs.

"They still considered it their factory," Murray says. "They felt that the five hundred dollars they had put into the co-op entitled them to be managers. They'd come to me and they'd say: 'In our factory we don't do this, we don't do that.'

"We had a bunch of young fellows in one department who felt from their parents' influence that this was their factory—and every so often, just like that, they'd pull a sit-down strike. Once, twice the foreman ran into my office, a few nasty words, and there was a sit-down strike. So I went out and I said to the boys: 'You'll have to go back to work and also fix any hats that are made bad!' They just turned their benches around away from the machines and just sat there.

"I stumped away from there for five minutes, and when I came back they're still sitting there.

"I said: 'Fellows, you're going to have to go back to work.'

"They wouldn't.

"I said: 'All right, you'll have to leave.'

" 'Sorry, we won't leave. This is our factory. You'll have to throw us out.' "

The way Murray tells it, he had to go to the mayor, who was also the judge, and get eighteen warrants for trespass. But the policeman, who was a local boy, wouldn't serve them.

"Murray," he said, "how can I do that? They're my friends."

Murray was in a spot. He had a factory to run, and here he was with his handful of perfectly legal warrants, and they were just so much paper. Murray called the State police. They told him they would be out right away; they would have liked nothing better.

But they never got the chance. The mayor and the policeman had been running around town, saying that this guy Greenbaum was going to give the Homesteads a black eye in the area, which was what the Homesteads needed least of all. And so the mayor and a delegation of citizens came to the factory, and there was a conference, and the trouble was straightened out before the State police could get there.

And after a time the hat factory began running normally, like any other factory, with grievances adjusted by bargaining between the union and the management. Which was fine for everybody, including the production of hats. Except that, when you look at it from the point of view of the town, it might well be considered an early, minor wound in the old spirit and the old meaning.

The hat factory continued in operation right through the war and up to the point when the government finally pulled out altogether in the late forties. But the change was there. When the war came, the younger men went into the Army and a lot of the rest, men and women, went into war industry for patriotic reasons, and maybe also because the pay was better. And Murray had to rummage around the area for help and even as far as New York City.

But then the war really changed everything in town, or at least it put the cap on changes that had been going on quietly, almost unnoticed, and made them permanent.

6

Nothing like a nice fat war to make prosperity. As the homesteaders found out.

All of a sudden there was more work than there were people to do it. A person could actually choose how he wanted to make a living and where.

A lot of people chose jobs out of town. Maybe some of them were tired of being stuck in one small place. Certainly it gave them a wonderful and quite new feeling that, for once in their lives, they were not in the minority. They were part of the war effort, as it was then called, the effort of the majority pulling together. For once they were being allowed to become part of the whole big country. This time it was the bigots and the Jew-baiters who had to keep their mouths shut and duck while they waved the flag and denied they had ever given money to the German-American Bund.

The sons of Jewish mamas went out into the war with a certain pride, I think. Each was given a farewell party and then he left, as if it were the most natural thing in the world that the tame child of a tame tailor (who may have been a draft evader from the Russian or Polish armies in his day) should go forth to shoot human beings and be shot at by them. According to the bronze plaque (fastened to a granite rock, for permanence, I suppose) sixty-four young men out of a population of about seven hundred put on a uniform and were shipped to parts unknown.

*

It was a time that is becoming hard to look back on. The enemy was the devil himself, and a mistake in policy did not yet threaten the extinction of life on earth. With Russia our ally, it was even all right to have been born in Kiev or Odessa.

There was money around. Automobiles were supposed to be hard to get, but there were more and more of them. Gas was rationed, but some people managed to finagle special ration stickers. They had to get to work at the defense plant in Trenton, didn't they? Most houses had telephones installed for the first time since they were built.

One phone in particular became the town's focus. The Civil Defense phone.

"We had to man the telephone alarm twenty-four hours a day," Ruby Ginsberg remembers. "It was connected with Red Bank, and we were to relay the message—you know, Red or Green or whatever color the alerts were—to Trenton, if we ever got one. It was all coded. For the whole war that phone never rang once. But it was taken very seriously. We were supposed to go to the old Borough Hall and sit there and wait for the phone to ring. Women in the daytime; men at night. People would drop in, drink coffee and kibbitz. Some took a book, some played poker. But it was all very serious.

"They had a detailed schedule, and you had to sign in and out to indicate that you had done your bit. One day I received a letter from the Council to report for dereliction of duty, and I realized I had forgotten my time. So I went to the meeting and there were three or four of us, and Mr. Gerson was one of them. Even then Mr. Gerson was one of the most religious and most orthodox Jews who never missed shul on the Sabbath and was very strict about all the observances. When we came in, there were a lot of dignitaries, the mayor and Nathan Gratz and several people from the Civil Defense in Trenton.

"I wanted to explain immediately that I was sorry and I would do anything I could, and then I wanted to go home. But

54

they wouldn't let me. I had to go through the whole procedure, four speakers including the Civil Defense people from Trenton.

"But before and during and after each man made his speech, Mr. Gerson kept raising his hand: he wanted to be heard.

"And the mayor kept saying: 'Not now, Gerson. Your turn will come.'

"Gerson kept repeating he had only a few words to say, but they were very stern and firm.

"So we had to sit there listening to all those people telling us how important the job was and the horrible thing we had done, breaking the chain, and all the awful things that could have happened as a result.

"And finally, after about an hour and a half of haranguing, Gerson raised his hand again. And they said, no, they were going to take me first because I had children to get back to.

"So I explained and apologized, and they bawled me out very gently, and, at last, it got to be Gerson's turn.

"He got up and in his timid voice he said: 'I wanted to tell you, I was there. I covered my turn. But it was Friday night, and you know that on a Friday night a good Jew isn't allowed to write. So I couldn't sign in or out.' "

Mr. Gerson is still around. I doubt that he goes anywhere except to shul, shuffling, bent over and very, very slowly. Each step costs him, you can see that, each shuffle is a separate undertaking requiring a separate and deliberate decision. Once a year, before Passover, he knocks at the door of our house to collect his annual dollar for matzos for the poor. And on his ruddy, ancient, boyish face he wears the remote and slightly mindless smile of the pious who have seen God.

As to Ruby, she's fiftyish and no small-town girl. Born in London and brought up in New York as the oldest daughter of a revolutionary Polish cloak-maker turned union organizer, she is married to a lawyer who represents employers in industrial disputes. She is well known in town for her gem-bright mind and her ability to laugh at anybody, herself included. She and her husband lived here all through the war.

"Those were the days," she tells, "when we had eight parties on every phone line. I'm frank to confess that on a boring day, if the phone would ring for somebody else, I'd pick it up to hear what was going on in town.

"Once I heard two ladies having a long discussion about their husbands.

"One of them, my neighbor, said: 'Gee whizz, I thought that when he went to work in a defense plant—he works so hard, all that overtime and everything—I thought he'd leave me alone. For Chrissake, he's worse than ever. I don't know what to do.'

"And the other girl says: 'I have practically the same trouble. I never can get through a night without him bothering me. . . .'

"The conversation was long and intimate. No detail left out, the approach and the rejection and the final acquiescence.

"I'll never forget the end:

"'It was good talking to you, Emma. One of these days we ought to get to know each other. . . .'"

Telephones, cars, V-mail letters from the boys in the service with long numbers for return addresses. The war was turning the town around from looking inward to reaching outward past Hightstown, past Trenton to distant islands in a vast tropical sea.

The reaching out is no figure of speech. The Homesteads were in the Philippines, Guadalcanal, Okinawa. Whoever figured out the numbers code, intended to conceal the location of the sender, hadn't counted on the ingenuity of the small-town mind.

Bill Perlmutter was in the Marines and this is what he has to say on the subject:

"We kept in touch with each other. We knew where everybody was. Everybody had a code. Besides, mail was censored going out, but it wasn't censored coming in. So some boy would write to his mother and she'd know where he was and then your mother would write to you and tell you where so-and-so was.

"I remember getting word that Ed Graditz's outfit was coming. So I went down and met him at the boat in Guadalcanal. I met him and we made a date, somewhere sixty miles down the island, and we'd meet halfway, three or four times, and then I didn't see him again for a year. I met Si Pinsker, he was in the Army, in rodent-control school learning to kill rats. He was living like a king in a beautiful tent with a wooden floor and screens on it, and I was living in the mud.

"Everybody hunted each other up, wherever they could. We knew where everybody was. I knew where Buck Alinsky was, in the Seabees, and Scratchy was in the Coast Guard, floating around in the Philippines. But there were only a few of us in the Pacific. Most everybody else went to Europe.

"And we in the Pacific also knew where everybody was in Europe. Manny Chernovsky's brother was a paratrooper over there, and I used to get V-mail from him, and he'd tell me where people were. There was continous mail flying back and forth."

The Homesteads were emptied of young men. All of them were in the service. All except Walter Weinberg, who kept showing up every once in a while at his parents' house for a brief visit. He had a job, the story went, out West where the Indians lived, in New Mexico. Why wasn't he in uniform? Such a healthy, husky boy in his business suit. There was a lot of talk about him and not a little resentment.

Like practically every other American town the Homesteads were being changed without anybody really knowing it. People felt themselves touching incredible places through their sons. Places like Anzio and Kwajalein and Tarawa. Who'd ever heard of them before? Or Corregidor, for that matter, where a boy from town was captured by the Japanese and perished on the Death March. The town suffered with him, went through an agony of hope when he was reported captured but alive, and grieved with his family on the news of his death in some inconceivable jungle. What a world! What a *new* world . . .

I sometimes wonder whether cars and telephones and money to pay for them, after a long, dragging period of being so desperately poor, might not have marked the start of that hunger for things—objects, gadgets—that has since come to characterize suburbia. Especially when deep worry was eating at people's innards, and the possession of possessions could be little more than a pipe dream, what with rationing and shortages of strategic materials.

In the meantime people planted victory gardens. Some of the older settlers knew how; a lot of the new ones, fresh from the city, made a mess of theirs. Just the same, when the tomatoes came in, the town drowned in tomatoes. The damned things ripened all at the same time. You couldn't give them away.

Most people followed government instructions. They saved old fat left over from cooking and took it to the store for shipment to some agency that collected it for re-use, God only knew for what. Also tin cans, stepped-on and flattened. And old newspapers. The Boy Scouts collected those. It was something to do, it made you feel a little less helpless, as though you were saying to the young men overseas: we don't know what they want with all this stuff we save, but we do it. If we didn't we'd feel even worse in our safety and comfort, with you out there in some mud hole where the Nazis throw shells at you and—God forbid—you might have to eat pork out of C-ration cans.

Nobody, nobody in town was against this war. I believe that.

There was griping, naturally, as there had to be. The war was an interminable bore, interrupted very rarely by short intervals of exhilaration or sudden and profound and impotent grief.

People got the news of FDR's death in various ways. A little kid heard the bulletin while listening to *Jack Armstrong, The All-American Boy,* and ran to tell mama. She, of course, had to run across the street to share what was, if true, unbearable for her alone. And the two of them ran to the neighbor's house. All over town the phones rang: husbands called wives from work and cried over the wire.

People drew together, friends with friends, and held on to each other, knocked over as by the unexpected death of a member of the family. The streets were empty. When a woman had to go to the store because she needed noodles for her soup, she spoke in whispers.

"The town," a man told me, "was sitting *shiva.*"

It took days for people to absorb the shock. FDR—everybody knew him personally from his pictures in the paper, from his Fireside Chats over the radio, from the newsreels in the movies— this man was much more than the commander in a war that involved them all. It was he who brought them out of the depression; without him there would have been no minimum wage, no Wagner Act, no social security; without him there would have been no Jersey Homesteads.

They held a memorial meeting. Nobody now seems to recall what went on in it. Perhaps they had been driven so deeply inward that nothing from the outside could make enough impression on them to cause them to remember.

Few had the guts to drive to Trenton to see the funeral train. Ben Shahn and Joe Ginsberg did go. And this is Joe's recollection:

"We were standing there on the platform when the train came in. We were standing there. And the train kept coming. And in front of us was a Negro man in his late seventies, and he started to heave. His shoulders kept moving up and down. He was sobbing so, neither of us could stand it. And we both broke up. And the train went through very slowly. . . ."

The future was pouring in on everybody. There was a sudden gap in time.

That very evening, as soon as he got home from Trenton, Ben started working on plans for a memorial to the dead president. He wanted it built in the open field near the school. He couldn't have known then what a job it was going to be to get people together and to raise the money. But he never gave it up for seventeen years until it was finally dedicated in the presence of Eleanor Roosevelt and assorted more or less appropriate dignitaries.

The changing of the town's name was much simpler: if anybody had objected (which I doubt) he wouldn't have dared to say so out loud.

Roosevelt, New Jersey: that was what it was now. When V-E day came, it drew a deep breath and went on a binge, an utterly unprecedented releasing of bottled-up feeling.

It started with a parade, a parade of cars. Every internal combustion vehicle that would move and had a horn got into it. They wound through the streets, tooting, blaring, again and again. Kids, wives and bystanders were squashed into them. Nobody minded, everybody was yelling and waving and throwing themselves around. Unlike most demonstrations, this one was really spontaneous.

And then the parties began. All-night parties unheard of up to then in this coffee-and-cake community where nobody ever raised his voice except to call a child or a dog or scream at somebody. At one house—and they collected in many houses—the owner tells me that more than a hundred people showed up, toting whatever drinkables they had put away for medicinal purposes: whiskey, gin, slivovitz, brandy.

"The next day we threw out twenty-six empties," the man told me. "Not counting beer."

What a catharsis! Grandpa Fleischman, with two boys in Europe, got drunk, went out and put his finger down his throat and came back to start all over again.

A schoolteacher, who normally set considerable store by his dignity, danced in the manner of Valentino. He grabbed the first handy girl and threw her over his shoulder and slid around in what was supposed to be a tango. The noise was formidable. And the kissing and hugging and the warm touching of others . . . Well, there wasn't a family in town which didn't have a son or a husband out there. And joy, after all, as well as misery, has need of company.

Everything afterwards was anticlimax. V-J day was accepted gratefully, especially by the families with boys in the Pacific. But it was expected, people were ready for it.

And the bombing of Hiroshima—nobody could grasp from one moment to the next what that was going to mean. A couple of days later Nagasaki. A big bomb? All right, a great big bomb. So what? It shortened the war, didn't it? It saved American lives, didn't it? As to Japanese lives, even in the hundred thousands, no one was in a mood to consider them.

One thing was clear all of a sudden, as soon as the more detailed newspaper accounts came out: what Walter Weinberg, the boy from Roosevelt who had never put on a uniform, had been doing all this time. People began to remember that he had a degree in physics, that he'd gone out to Chicago and then moved to New Mexico. Well—it didn't take a genius to put two and two together and get Los Alamos.

7

"I remember it explicitly," Bill Perlmutter says. "Getting a letter from home telling me that I now lived in a town with another name. I didn't want anything to change. When I got home I wanted everything to be just the way I left it.

"I got home in February of '46, and the town and the houses looked drab and cold and miserable. I was in uniform, and I remember coming down the street, and a few women ran up to me and shook my hand. And I didn't know who they were. I had grown up with them around, and I'd been gone only three years, and I didn't recognize any of them. One woman in particular, when I went past her house, she came out and grabbed hold of me and welcomed me. And she ran ahead of me to tell my mother I was coming. And afterwards, when everything quieted down, I had to ask my mother who she was. I just didn't know."

The rest of the men—they could hardly be called boys anymore—may not have had as stubborn a memory as Bill's. They floated into town over the next couple of months, and for each homecoming there was a party. Which made a lot of parties. And later there was this thing called civilian life. Which for most of them meant a decent job and a little money in the bank and getting married, if they weren't already.

Maybe Bill had an extraordinary loyalty to his own personal fiction of his childhood and adolescence (the sort everyone carries around in himself, more or less well stowed and more or less important). Perhaps this caused him to demand that nobody and nothing should grow older while he was being put through boot training and murder on the beaches. Not people. Not even trees. Any change, growth or decay, made them other than his own and therefore unrecognizable.

It amounted to a fanatical insistence on what life ought to be like in America, I suppose, and specifically in his town. The sort of fanaticism that was then (and still is) common throughout the country and most virulently in the veterans' organizations. With Hitler and Tojo disposed of and the great depression overcome, change itself became the enemy. And in town change was inescapable.

Not only were there lots of new people who never had anything to do with making the community what it used to be and who hadn't shared in its own particular hard times; worse, the government had made up its collective mind to get out of the resettlement business and was ready to force the settlers to buy their houses if they wanted to stay in them.

None of this was on the surface. There was no way for Bill to see it, walking into town as he did. Something must have happened inside of him, somehow his love and his well-hidden fear must have gotten mixed up. And he couldn't allow that; it was far better not to recognize what didn't match.

But the war was a watershed. Not just in town; all over the big world. And whether you were willing and able to recognize the newness in all its many meanings, you had no choice, you had to eat it and swallow it, even if it made you sick.

There was a huge hullabaloo about the houses. It was not hard to see that, with an expensive school to keep up and a municipal water and sewage system to maintain—not to mention streets and police and equipment for the volunteer fire company— the cost of living in town was going to jump, once the government was gone. The residents gave the usual excellent account of themselves: Washington knew it had been in a fight by the time the last of many delegations had raised hell with every administrative officer and politician they could get at. But the forces were too unequal: the houses were sold to the tenants—at a low price and on the easiest terms, it was true—but they were sold and they had to be bought.

It is my idea that at least some of the homesteaders must have sensed that what they were struggling against was much more far-reaching than any mere expenditure of money: this was the close-out sale, and they and their town were being abandoned, with the governmental umbrella removed, to a cold rain of reality. And what the future was going to bring, nobody could tell.

And several of them started huddling together in small protective groups, with their separateness pulled around themselves, and more than a little suspicious of everybody else.

It was about that time that Sam and Grace Morgenstern moved into town. Sam had recently been brought from New York to work as an executive for a company that manufactured lamps in Freehold; he was living in a rented room and he was looking for a house nearby where he could live decently with his wife and his two children. In the factory he ran into Sidney Hess who suggested that he should look into Roosevelt. Sid did more than that: he found a suitable house for the Morgensterns. They moved in and loved it, and that was the beginning of a friendship.

"The day I met Bertha Hess," Grace says, "she took hold of me, like so, you know, and I felt, how wonderful, I'm going to have a very good friend. She introduced me to Hannah Silver, who was my neighbor, and to Nettie Warshawski. And these three were very close friends, and now suddenly they got a new one—me. They took me in, and for months I didn't realize that I wasn't seeing a soul except these people. I had absolutely no freedom to do anything I wanted. They said there wasn't anybody else in town worth knowing, and, stupid us, we were so gullible, we believed it for months."

Now, it simply isn't true that Sam is stupid, far from it. A short, rotund man given to large cigars, he's had a number of responsible jobs in town and out, and people tend to listen when he gives his opinion. They also listen to his jokes, of which he has an inexhaustible supply. But, being a big-city man, he was not prepared for the involutions of small-town life, as they soon became evident in this very singular village.

As to Grace, she loves catering "affairs" for worthy causes

and organizations. Her bread-and-butter pickles and garlic almonds are well known to her friends, because she gives jars of them away whenever she can find a remotely suitable occasion. Her household arts seem to be part of a view of life learned, no doubt, in the Bronx where she grew up in total respectability; she holds all the permanent values, and when she knows beforehand that a movie contains overt premarital sex, she won't go to see it.

Even today in her late middle age, she is easily taken in and easily hurt: she is still, I am afraid, almost as trusting as she must have been when she first arrived. But she runs her family with what Ben Shahn used to call a whim of iron. As can be seen from the following:

"Bertha would call me right after breakfast, as soon as the kids were off to school, and she'd say: 'What are you doing?' And I'd have to tell her what I was doing. And I'd have to be finished with my housework no later than two o'clock because that was when we had the coffee klatch. If I'd get sleepy from the country air I wasn't used to, I'd get the 'coffee ready' signal just the same, right on time. Ever since we started living here I was having terrible heartburn from all that coffee. And when Sam came home we would have supper and we would all get together again. The same people. But the kids were loving it here, mainly, I sometimes think, because we got them a dog.

"Anyway, one winter day I had to walk Toni to school. There was a lot of ice and the street was slippery. And Mrs. Abrams from across the street comes out of her house and says to me: 'Grace, I'm afraid to walk on the ice, so could I walk with you and hold you?' So I said: 'Of course, come on'; and we walked to school. And I come back and I get in the house and the telephone rings and it's Bertha Hess.

" 'What were you doing with the Abrams woman, going to school with her?'

"I said that she asked me if she could walk with me because she was afraid of the ice.

"Bertha said: 'She's not afraid of the ice, she's just trying to get you to be her friend.'

"I hung up and I said to myself: 'My God, what's with me?

How stupid can you get? She's not letting us meet anybody.' And I decided that this couldn't go on.

"A couple of nights later Sam came home, and I said: 'I can't stand it anymore, the same conversation over and over again. I don't get a chance to make other friends. I want to go back to New York.' The kids heard me say it, and they carried on something terrible. But I said: 'Well, I tell you, if we don't move back to New York, I'm going to have a nervous breakdown.'

"Well, Sam found an apartment and the night before we went back to the city, there was a party for us, and for the first time we met a lot of other nice people, Ben included, but then there was no way out, we had to go. Everybody said: 'What are you leaving this town for?' And I thought to myself, oh, I feel terrible, and Sam and the kids were miserable.

"I had never lived in an apartment before, even in the Bronx we had a private house. And six weeks after we started living in that New York apartment I suddenly got hysterical. Here I was looking out on the side of a building and I thought to myself, what did I do? What did I do? I didn't dare tell Sam. Here we had a lease for a year, and the kids were miserable, absolutely miserable.

"So we started coming back on visits every weekend, and finally we came back to stay. By then we had made lots of friends, all except the original group. They considered us traitors. We had gone over to the Reds, they said."

The Reds? Who were the Reds? Surely the two or three open communists in town, trying to sell subscriptions to the *Daily Worker* (mailed in a plain wrapper), weren't frightening anybody. So they went on their demonstrations for their latest approved cause. So let them.

"You don't know them," the answer went. "They're devious, they hide, they bore from within. You never can tell who—it might be the mother of your child's best friend, it might be your neighbor. You never know. . . ."

It was a time when suspicion of one's neighbor was emerging as a national neurosis. Crew-cut investigators in identical gray suits kept sniffing around the post office and Frenchy's gas station and hunting for individuals with a grudge, digging for rumors.

Some goyish farmers in the area went so far as to say that maybe we'd been fighting on the wrong side all along. Where there was that much smoke, there had to be some fire.

There was a sense of a new war before the criminals of the last war were hanged in Nuremberg. No less than Mr. Churchill himself made it clear in that speech in—what was the name of the place out in Missouri? A person had to be careful whom he was seen with. Or in front of whose house he parked his car.

"This was right after the war," Bertha explains. "There was a saying at the time, you had to ask yourself: 'Is he a communist or is he a traveler?' Being that Sid worked for the government in the accounting department, you see, he wasn't allowed to participate with travelers."

It is quite clear what Bertha meant when she said "traveler." But I wonder whether there may not have been another less apparent meaning in her use of the word, a connotation of oddball, of the not entirely kosher—of what in other, more average communities would have been labeled "foreigner." Could it be that in a time of pressure and confusion she and her little ingrown clique were made especially uneasy by a new small bunch of outsiders whose ways of being and of making a living were so utterly mysterious, and whose private lives and motivations were therefore even more suspect than those of the old-time, once familiar neighbors whom she was suddenly no longer able to trust?

It was true, this particular lot of newcomers weren't much of a threat: they were no more than five or six families altogether. They could have been safely ignored, it would seem. But they didn't go to work like respectable people, they didn't ride the commuter train out of Princeton Junction. Instead they stayed home most of the time, doing what they felt like doing. And if they did go to New York, they'd take the ten o'clock like the bosses and the bankers. Where did they get their money?

Every once in a while they'd have visitors from the city, and you could never foretell what kind of car these visitors might be driving, a new Caddy or a busted-down Chevvy, prewar vintage. Some of them might look like judges, others like bums. . . . And the singing that went on in those homes, and the drinking and the loud arguments that sounded as if they were going to kill each other—it was bound to make gossip. Besides, from what they'd say and from the way they carried on, it didn't take an expert to figure out that every one of them must have been what the government men referred to as premature antifascists.

Some were book writers, others were artists like Ben Shahn. Only they weren't like him either. Most weren't even Jewish. What brought them? What made them pick this town out of the hundreds they could have picked? Ben Shahn must have had something to do with it. At that time a lot of people were beginning to suspect that Ben might be a Red or at least a "traveler."

It should be remembered that by war's end Ben's position had changed significantly. His name got in the paper often, not just in the *Times,* in the Jewish press too. But in town he was still the ordinary man everybody knew and fought with, who had arrived years ago almost as poor as a cloak-maker. If he was more prosperous now—well, so were most people.

As Stella (who knew both Ben and the settlers as well as anyone) puts it: "Ben was no more vigorous than they were. They could be just as dominant and powerful and idea-proud as he was. Don't forget that they had gotten to America with nothing and had made a life and now were sending their kids to college. By their lights they were wildly successful."

But to the handful of other artists arriving in town Ben became the mountain to climb. If he could draw out of this little place the energy to grow into the champion social painter of his period—well, maybe they could do the same. A simplistic notion? Probably. But understandable.

As for Ben himself, he wallowed in the feeling of being the center of the room. He learned to expect people to laugh at his stories. (It seemed that his anecdotes had become part of an automatic mechanism in him that could be triggered by the right word from anyone who knew him well enough. Say the word, and the story came, like a chocolate bar out of a candy machine after you put a dime in the slot.)

Some years later our little daughter (she must have been about six at the time) asked Ben if he was famous.

"I don't know," Ben told her. "Fame is like a smudge on your nose. You can't see it. Only other people can."

But Ben could see it, I am sure of that.

He was exceptionally gregarious. Something drove him out of his house at night to go visiting, alone and unannounced. The door would open, and there he would be, friendly, convivial and big as a bear. Often he'd stay late, making talk, smoking, drinking coffee. It was as though he required another intimacy, after a day spent in his own home and studio; as though he had to touch lives a step removed from his own.

Art, he often said, can't survive isolation. The artist may work in total aloneness. But the ordinary has to be there for him when he's finished. He has to swim in it like a fish in water. Take him out, and he shrivels. . . . How much this theory had to do with his nightly wanderings, I cannot tell.

I do know that at town parties he invariably stayed to the bitter end. As though he were afraid he might miss something. He held court. The younger people—the children of the settlers and some of the better-educated commuters—clustered around him. They were, I think, eager to pick up bits of information about this art-thing which could, they had been told, enlarge a person in his own view and in the opinion others had of him. Besides, Ben was fun, when he wanted to be challenging, if you got into an argument with him. True, he could be rude. And condescending. But never dull.

Yet, as an audience these cultural innocents could hardly be enough for Ben. Talking to them was too much like teaching class. If he was going to stay in town—and on balance he did want to stay—he had to make the effort to attract at least a few individuals who didn't require an accounting of how much it cost an artist to tear his images out of himself like aching teeth. The first such import was Stuart Hotchkiss.

Stuart was a natural choice. A sculptor and ceramist, he had worked with Ben during the war and he was Ben's ardent admirer. (A prerequisite, no doubt.) But in this town, Stuart was totally exotic, a creature out of another dimension, a character out of romantic fiction. And his long-range effect was incalculable.

Stuart was a gallant, a lover of the ladies (almost any would do if the moment was right), a spender of money he didn't always

68

have; also the husband of a sad, once beautiful wife and the father of two charming, blond and very goyish-looking boys.

It was hard to dislike Stuart: he was so open and cheerful. And he was a superlative host. He soon changed the whole character of social intercourse among the members of the younger set. He was a catalyst, dropped into the town at the right time. He brought home to the elders that their children were grown-up and that a lot of them were not going to continue in the old ways. Particularly some of the young women who had followed the prescribed line into marriage, had born their allotment of children, and now, awakened by Stuart, realized that they had missed a lot of life. They weren't immigrants: they were the children of immigrants, which is very different. Unsatisfied by what their parents had achieved with such tremendous effort, they had been too frightened to break out from the tight grip of the old, safe values to taste for themselves the glamour of the big city. For them Stuart was made to order.

"He had an attitude," Stella comments, thinking back, "that was quite different from the mama-laden Jewish boys who were marriage-oriented and couldn't accept sexual relationships without getting all punitive with themselves and whomever they were sleeping with. He was attractive and he had a taste for the high life. There was no burden in going with him. He owed you nothing and you owed him nothing. All there was to it was a good time and lovely luxury. He would take these dames out to places and do things that these depression-reared women had never experienced. For them it was like being let out of a cage. . . ."

For a lot of them, I guess; but not Stuart's wife. She had learned long before that no woman, and she least of all, could hold Stuart for long. Not in those days. . . . If any of the husbands minded, they made no public fuss.

Of course none of this could have happened with so little repercussion, if the girls hadn't been so ready for it. It is almost impossible to imagine now the passionate longing of adolescent girls for the sophisticated urban pleasures, locked away as the girls were in their inaccessible provincial town.

"I was just out of high school," Stella says, "and I had a friend who was older. She couldn't have been more than twenty, but she was married and she already had a baby. Her husband was working nights, and so she and I spent a lot of evenings together at her house. In their garden they had planted a lot of purple cabbages, and they were very beautiful.

"So she and I would go out there and say: 'What a beautiful color!' And then we'd say: 'Wouldn't it be nice to have a couch that color.' So then we started planning a room around this purple-cabbage couch. And we got into this elaborate fantasy game, going way beyond that room. We started planning a whole life. And we would say: 'We should have a town house in New York, one of those brownstones.' And we planned how it should look. I was going to be married by then (I don't know to whom) and we were going to be living together in this house. We didn't want to do any housework, and we'd get into these long discussions, like, should we have a maid and where she would live and the kind of parties we'd have, and our discomfort at having anybody wait on us whom we couldn't ask to sit down with the guests. So we finally decided against the maid. . . . We talked about the furnishings of the house and the kind of posh entertaining we would do, and the looking around the city we wanted to do and the kind of clothes we would wear. It went on for weeks. And it was all based on these purple cabbages."

What finally happened between the purple-cabbage lady and the increasingly middle-aged artist chasing careless youth is of small importance to the biography of a town. So they had their flaming affair; so they broke up just as soon as she had left her husband and moved, beckoning, to an apartment in New York. So . . . There wasn't too much fuss. Stuart was O.K. After all he was only doing what was expected of him in accordance with the stereotype of the irresponsible bohemian as it was projected daily in what was then not yet called "the media." Stuart confirmed a universal prejudice. And, no matter what a man may do, such confirmation is always reassuring.

Stuart's relations with the townspeople were smoother than might have been anticipated. He organized free art lessons for housewives. And he could be counted on if any of their husbands needed help in building a table or a bookcase. He was so free of bigotry that his two sons didn't realize they weren't like the Jewish kids until they got to Hightstown High, where they were abruptly enlightened. It was easy to forgive him for driving a long, low, racy Cord automobile that was forever getting stuck on the high center of the local dirt roads and had to be pulled out; and if he wanted to brag about his conquest of a female piano player in a nightclub, there was, I believe, more envy than disapproval in the reaction of most residents.

His parties were something radically new: colored lights in the garden, shishkebab and charcoal-broiled chicken, music, dancing on the lawn and fancy liquor, any amount of it—Hollywood in Roosevelt. All sorts of fascinating out-of-towners showed up—singers, crazy writers with wild ideas, once in a while a celebrity: the singing (on a loudspeaker or live) and the abandoned gaiety kept going from early evening to the following morning, when overpowering breakfasts were consumed alfresco in the heavy New Jersey mist.

The younger set started to imitate Stuart in their entertaining (within or slightly beyond their means), trying to be modern sophisticates when in fact they were forerunners of the suburban Saturday night. Except that there was still an innocence about the whole phenomenon: Stuart himself, the son of a Middle Western Methodist clergyman in revolt against the puritan ethic, had no idea, I'm sure, that he was acting the pitchman for the full-blown consumer society just around the corner of history to come.

Some of the side effects were pretty funny. Jules Goldblatt tells about one of them:

"I suppose you've heard the stories about the joint breakfasts —no?" Jules begins. "At one point, maybe because Frenchy at the gas station was getting hard to take or because the papers weren't coming through, we decided to buy our Sunday *Times* in Hightstown. Four or five of us, Ben, Stuart and Doug Miller and ourselves and I don't remember who else. We set it up alphabetically so that each week one guy would drive to Hightstown and buy five papers and deliver them all around. The trouble was, you couldn't just go into the Shahn house and drop your paper and go. You had to have a cup of coffee and a little chat. So, by the time you delivered the fifth paper, it was about six o'clock and the guy was bloated, and the people were furious: Where you been with my paper all day?

"So we decided that instead of the one guy delivering the paper—the other four or five would come to his house and have coffee. So it was nice, eh? You would think so, wouldn't you? Not if you know Roosevelt, you wouldn't.

"So the first one maybe was Goldblatt. So they came in and had coffee. And the next time, in addition to coffee we'd have some Danish pastry. The second one, maybe, was Hotchkiss, and you know Stuart was a sport, so we had coffee and eggs and toast. You can see it coming, can't you? The third one, Miller, did something crazy—I think he made *latkes*. Then the Shahns had kippers. My next time around I went to Trenton, and there's a little Jewish section there, and I went in and bought lox and bagels and bialys and black olives and sour cream. Well, after a few times around the lady and gentleman whose turn it was would sit down on Saturday night to make up a menu.

"It ended as it had to end, with Stuart Hotchkiss, who was the biggest sport of all. He bought fancy china, Rosenthal or something like that, and they had their beautiful table all freshly waxed, and we had kippers and lox, and Mary prepared onion omelettes, and there were seven kinds of bread and wine and brandy, and the thing lasted all day and it got to be a bash. We couldn't keep it up anymore. The next day was going to be Monday, which was bad enough without a hangover. . . ."

It was, you might say, a minor culinary attempt to keep up with the Joneses.

In the meantime, while this sort of high jinks was going on in one small sector of the community, the town, seen superficially, seemed to be riding along on old habits: meeting-going and fighting over nothing were pleasures not easily relinquished; neither were coffee klatches and gossip, nor listening in on party-line telephone calls. Those were the days when a Board of Education meeting could still fill the big school lobby under Ben's mural. One memorable evening two respectable board members throwing insults at each other over the matter of the cut-off date for admission of five-year olds, got into a brawl and rolled around on the floor until one tore the shirt off the other's back. I don't know whether coffee and homemade cake was served afterwards by the ladies of the PTA.

Smallness was as small as ever. And there were more than enough old settlers left to make for continuity in patterns of behavior and especially in the overriding feel of sitting in the same round co-operative pot: when a settler's daughter showed signs of getting married, the whole town acted as though she were everybody's child. Political differences and growing suspicion notwithstanding.

Stella wrote to Goldie from the West Coast where she was working: "Mama, I've met a nice young man, but don't go telling anybody I'm engaged."

Goldie, of course, read this as: "Mama, I'm engaged but don't tell anybody." And she immediately called a friend and told her: "Stella's engaged, but don't tell anybody, she doesn't want people to know."

I have no information how long it took for the news to travel through town—somewhere between a half hour and an hour, I would estimate.

In any case, when Stella brought Milton for a visit sometime later, he had to undergo the usual inspection reserved for potential husbands of nice Jewish girls—only here it was not limited to the fiancée's immediate family, it extended to the whole village, everyone felt he had a stake in the transaction.

"Well, you know, I was really on review when I first came here," Milton recalls. "I had just graduated from Chicago after spending some years as an engineer in the merchant marine, and Stella and I had agreed that it would be a good idea for me to check out the town. Since, obviously, it had to be a package deal if we got married—the town came with Stella.

"I had a marvellous black 1943 Buick convertible then, with red leather upholstery that had once belonged to the president of Western Airlines. My friends called it the 'super-pussy-wagon.' Two merchant seamen who had gone through Berkeley with me and an Iranian girl and Stella and I steamed into town in the splendid Buick. And, no sooner had we arrived at Stella's house, when people began dropping in. First Gratz, then other people. I remember the Shahns paid us a visit. And there I was on display.

The town looked kind of bare to me, but pleasant. It had the sense of community I liked so much on ships."

How the tongues must have waggled, how Milton must have been dissected! A serious young man, but what kind of work is that, engineer on a boat? He'll be away six months at a time. What'll that do to the children?

Milton left the merchant marine before long: he's a city planner now and commutes to Asbury Park. And the marriage has lasted these many years in spite of the town and because of it, both—and for many other reasons, certainly, that I know nothing about.

It was a time when a lot of people in town started worrying about jobs again. With the war over, was there going to be another depression? What was this thing the papers called automation? Nearly everybody was still working. But was it going to last?

Never in the short history of the republic (and the even shorter interval since the old settlers had any part in it) was the shape of the future so difficult to make out for an ordinary person. What was a computer? Could it really think like a man? Was it maybe going to replace the garment workers at their sewing machines? And, if an atom bomb were to hit New York, was the fallout going to reach Roosevelt?

What was needed was another New Deal, only bigger and better. Roosevelt was one of the few localities where Henry Wallace's Progressive Party carried the 1948 election, with Truman close behind and Dewey almost nonexistent. The issue here was not between Republicans and Democrats: it was between moderates and radicals of the same persuasion. And the politicking, as always, was participatory as hell.

Both sides held meetings and both sides threw cause parties. It got so bad that kids who were adolescent at the time were baffled when they were invited to a party that was just for fun: what was the party for, they wanted to know, and had their dimes and quarters ready in their hands.

The intellectuals—and those who wanted to be known as such—were out in front of the local Progressive Party campaign. Ben painted posters which got national attention. One of them, caricaturing Truman playing the piano for Dewey, was to become a collector's item. And Stuart's cause parties were said to be so fabulous that members of the opposition were tempted to show up.

They didn't, of course. It would have been treason.

Treason was the word then. It was, you will recall if you are old enough, the period of the spy trials. The enemy sat not only in Moscow and Peking and Greece and East Berlin, but in Washington and, naturally, New York, and, for all anybody could tell, in a coffee shop in Keokuk, Iowa. How could a Jewish town that had voted as this one did, escape suspicion?

A Hightstown acquaintance told me about it:

"I remember my stepfather saying: 'Those pinkos in Roosevelt, those Reds,' and all that stuff," he recalled. "And I'd say: 'Don't say that. You don't know what you're talking about. There's nothing wrong with those people, how do you know they're communists?' And he'd say that it all came out during the war. Somebody ran an FBI man off the road. An FBI man had gone out there to investigate and somebody had run him off the road with a car and killed him. Folks believed that."

Nearly everyone in town could feel the hostility, it was closing in all around. And those who didn't, got to thinking they did from the stories that some commuters brought home, especially men with a business somewhere else. Stanley Reiss was one of those:

"I had a little business down the shore near Point Pleasant around 1946 to '51," Stanley says. "In those days, before they got to know me better, they would ask me where I was from. And the minute I told them Jersey Homesteads, and then gave them my address: 16 North Co-operative Circle, the whole bit, they'd say: 'Isn't that the town full of communists?'

"You see, those clam-diggers knew about us; they'd dug the foundations and laid the pipes. They were the mechanics and the artisans on WPA, and so they knew. And if you said Jersey Homesteads, you were a dead duck. They knew it was Jewtown, and they wouldn't hesitate to say: 'All the communists come from there.'

"They would stand there and say it to you, period.

"I was happy to be able to say—after it was changed to Roosevelt, and people asked me where I lived—'I live in Roosevelt. A town a little bit west of Freehold and a little bit near Hightstown.' But it didn't help much. They'd say: 'Oh, wasn't that called Jersey Homesteads?' They wouldn't forget it.

"All I could do was wind up those hawks a little bit and say: 'My name is Stanley Reiss and I happen to be a Democrat and normal as apple pie. I fought in the war, I salute the flag and I love America, and please—please get out of my way.'"

Now, Stanley gets carried away when he talks. He didn't exactly fight in any war. He told me so himself when he was running on about how clever he had been during his years in the Army, to keep the military from sending him overseas. But that's Stanley—the words spill out of him, and you're not supposed to take him literally.

Stanley has a fleshy face with small eyes punched in it and a walrus mustache. He started the kids' drum-and-bugle corps in town, and on patriotic occasions he marches ahead of the ten-year olds (who squeak and croak unmercifully, to the delight of their mamas) and he precedes them as solemnly as if they were an elite corps of paratroopers. If he tells somebody that he fought in the war, he's not lying. What he means is: I'm a good Joe just like you; I believe in the same things other good Americans believe in. In 1950 or '51 he was the perfect choice for leadership in the newly formed Civic League.

The Civic League was an organization specifically intended to clear the town of Reds, although this purpose did not appear in so many words in its bylaws. To quote Stanley once more:

"We formed the Civic League to cleanse ourselves of this thing, and for heaven's sake to take our place in Monmouth County as a borough instead of being given a special title. Unless it was a good one, like you say New Hope is noted for its lovely art—right?—or the Bronx Zoo for its fourteen striped zebra. That would be OK, but when you get around to Roosevelt, the best we could hope for was that it was a town loaded with communists, or worse yet, Jew-communists. That was it.

"Sure, we were loaded with Jews, God bless 'em. They happened to be Jews because a poodle dog is a poodle dog. But, of course, so far as communists were concerned, one can make a choice. The most important thing to us was to get rid of that slur. Out in the business world we could go miles away, and boy, I want to tell you, it stopped you cold. There were many instances when they walked away and said: 'Oh, well—let's not deal with this communist.' "

The organization was, of course, not limited to businessmen with contacts to make. It must have had sixty or seventy members at five bucks a membership, and it contained the frightened as well as the angry, old and young, and very many who wanted more than anything to be submerged in America. Even if it was the America of Joe McCarthy.

Bernarda Shahn recently characterized the Civic League to me—with benefit of hindsight and the elapsed years—as a spell of unimportant Jewish fascism.

At the time it couldn't be taken so lightly. It even published a monthly paper, the *Civic League Reporter*. And in as small a town as this one, words became ice picks: people were hurt.

Not all the members were as insensitive as Stanley to the damage being done to human beings whom, until the formation of the League, they had thought of as people with good points and bad points, but always as fellow-townsmen. And some of these now beat their breasts before anyone who will listen. People like Si Pinsker.

"It was a pretty lousy situation," Si says. "You know it was the McCarthy type of thing and we were sucked into it. We went out of our way to hurt people. We were pretty bitchy, let me tell you. . . . I've changed, but some of the people have not. . . . It wasn't important if somebody was a communist or not, whether he was a card-holder or not. We were such little people that a difference of opinion was enough for us. We didn't need more than that to condemn somebody. You didn't need to prove him wrong to condemn him. It was blind. It was childish. . . . But look, I can't evade the facts. I was there. And the only thing I can say for myself is that I was one of the youngest. Me, I was a follower, but I had a big mouth, so I thought I was leading. I was being a big fish in a little bowl, and I really thought I had things going for me. I was used. It took me a long while to learn and I hope I've learned. I don't know. But Ben and Alvarado and Sam Morgenstern, who became my friends later—they were the scapegoats. We brutalized these people with no reason whatsoever. We did them a terrible disservice.

"And Ben fought. In his own way he fought. He'd get angry, oh boy! He'd get so pissed. And yet he'd have his sense of humor.

"Once we had a meeting and he walked in on us. The room was pretty full of people. And he sat down to listen. He didn't say anything. He was as sweet as anything. Just sat down. I tell you there must have been fifty or sixty people in that room, and there wasn't a single one of us in that crowd who had enough guts to stand up and say: 'Ben, get the hell out! This thing is against you!' None of us had the spunk. The man had enough guts to come in and tackle us all in his own quiet, pleasant little manner. He beat us. By just being there he beat us."

The Civic League is long gone, but many of its members remain in town, and some of them, like Si, wish they could forget all about it. But in a few of us here there is, I think, a sneaking fear that if it could happen once it might happen again, even in this village where we are all so closely tied together, if the hysteria should start all around us again, as some think it is about to do right now. Because who ever really learns anything?

8

The Civic League went out of business before the end of 1952. After all, hating takes as much energy as loving. And organized hating gets to be a chore when you keep bumping into The Enemy at the post office and need to borrow his lawn mower.

I imagine that the whole thing was just too uncomfortable to live with day after day: even though the terrors of the Rosenberg case and the Korean war and Joe McCarthy hunting subversives were enough to further frighten the adherents of the true and tried and therefore imperishable American Way.

The trouble was, in town, that nobody quite knew what to do with the dead body of a hate organization. It embarrassed both sides. The stink of it, made up of leftover angers and slowly decomposing hurt feelings, continued hanging in the country air.

And the questions the League had raised that now lay wide-open! Such as: Whom could you trust? What was friendship worth? Could the split community be glued together again without leaving a visible crack?

The crack was certainly still there when we arrived in the spring of 1953. We didn't see it right away, you understand. To us the town seemed exceptionally peaceful and friendly and hospitable. Which goes to show how unreliable first impressions can be. Or maybe not. Maybe our first look came closer to the truth than our later, more informed appreciation.

We had been away from this continent for seven years when we arrived. All our connections were loosened by our stay on an island—Puerto Rico, to be specific—which tends to see the whole world in terms of itself even more than does Roosevelt, New Jersey. Not that we could help feeling a certain spill-over of remote events, as we felt the boom of the great waves at the end of the street where we lived, rolling in on a sunny day from a storm around a very distant center.

Now we were returning to that center, and it wasn't easy. The month was April, and a lot of trees were not yet in leaf, and that was enough to make us apprehensive: we hadn't seen a change of season in all our years in the tropics, and naked trees sticking into cold, low skies, looked—to me at least—like the skeletons of hands. Our concept of home was dislocated. We had had two children (both girls) on the island and we had left friends there; bougainvillea and hibiscus had got to seem more natural to us than forsythia and early, timid tulips. And we had lost contact with most of the group we had known earlier in New York and Washington. We couldn't even write to them that we were coming back and needed a place to stay. We had no idea of what had happened to them or where they lived.

Except for Ben and Bernarda: we knew they were in Roosevelt. And this knowledge brought us: with two kids parked in the too-small house of a sister-in-law on the Jersey shore, we had to find a home in a hurry.

Bernarda seemed delighted. Before we came she wrote us a long hymn about the town, and she located a house for us, the one we are still living in. As soon as we saw it, we realized that it was in superperfect shape. The truck driver and his wife (particularly the wife) who had preceded us must have petted and polished it until it literally shone. There were so many coats of paint on the walls that, if you had measured the rooms, each would have been an inch smaller than its original dimension. The couple's children, we were told by the wife, as though this were the most natural thing in the world, had been allowed in the house only in their stocking feet and carrying their shoes.

"I didn't want them dragging mud in from the street," she

explained, not without pride. She was a smooth-faced, bulky woman, and you could see that she took at least two baths a day.

But what colors! The living room was appalling in deep purple, dark as a dungeon because the blinds and curtains were kept firmly shut—probably for years—to prevent the rugs and upholstery from fading in the daylight. One of the bedrooms, if I remember it correctly, was a dismal sort of green. A certain detail sticks vividly in my recollection: a fake fireplace without flue pasted against a wall and furnished with andirons and simulated logs. If anyone had taken it seriously the house would have gone up in flames. It's funny now. It was a little terrifying then. Into what kind of benighted village had we blundered?

Of course there was Ben, and he was cordial, happy to have us. As soon as our furniture arrived he gave us a very handsome, large, framed print, inscribed: "To Louise and Ed—Welcome."

While our title deed was being searched and the house was scraped and repainted white, I got acquainted with the town. Several times, while driving around, I got lost. The houses were so much alike. But everybody I met leaned over backwards to be friendly. I stayed with people I had never seen before, and they wouldn't hear of accepting money from me. All of which softened the effect on me of the box houses and the drab, flat landscape.

Of course I wanted to like the place. I knew I had to: the papers for the house were beyond recall. And Ben Shahn took time out from his work to drive me around the countryside. He showed me odd old fretwork houses within a few miles of town and spoke of them possessively, as though he owned them. He took me to Crosswicks and pointed out a huge oak tree dating from the time of William Penn. In his own way he was being a guide for a tour of one. I was touched: it didn't occur to me that he might have urgencies of his own that made our settling in Roosevelt worth his trouble.

When he wanted, Ben could be hypersensitive to what was going on in someone else. He must have felt how hard I found it to relate to this environment. He tried to help and, as usual, he did it with an anecdote.

"I had to go to the city a couple of weeks ago," he said while we drove along one of the winding back roads. "I had to see my gallery and I stopped in at the office of a damn fool art director who'd sent me a trashy story to illustrate for his magazine.

" 'Thanks just the same,' I told him. 'I don't want to do it.'

" 'What's the matter, Ben?' he said. 'We can discuss the fee.'

" 'The pay is fine,' I told him. 'It's the story.'

" 'What's the matter with the story?'

" 'It's vulgar,' I told him.

"Well—you should have seen his face! An artist turning down a fat fee because he didn't like a story. . . .

" 'What'll I tell my editor?' he said.

" 'Tell him, when he sends me a decent story, I'll be glad to illustrate it,' I said.

"Well, when he saw that I wasn't going to budge, he started buttering me up. I guess he wanted to keep on good terms for future reference. You know how it is—an art director is only as good as the artists he can get to work with him. So we talked. Now, you must understand that this was the kind of idiot who has three martinis before lunch and a couple more in the club car on his ride back to Westport, Connecticut.

"And he says to me: 'Ben,' he says, 'why don't you move out to Westport too?'

" 'I like it where I am,' I said.

" 'Come on,' he says. 'You're a big boy now, why don't you dig yourself out of the Jersey meadows?'

" 'I like it down there,' I said, 'because it's flat.'

"He looked at me as if I was crazy. 'What's wrong with hills?' he said.

"I was putting on my overcoat and was getting ready to walk out of that plush office, and I turned around and I told him.

" 'Nothing wrong with hills,' I told him. 'Only I like to see the horizon across honest-to-goodness crops. Come down some time and I'll show you what honest country is. No gentlemen farmers, only real ones, with dirt under their fingernails. And no art directors at all.'

"I laughed with him at his punch line, although I didn't exactly feel like laughing. Maybe one day I was going to fit into this place, not as Ben seemed to fit into it, probably, but somehow.

Maybe I too was going to learn to love and admire sere brown fields and gray sky. But not right after seven years in the company of steep, green, tropical mountains and a picture-postcard sea.

Finally the day came when our furniture was due to arrive. Louise and I had slept on the floor of the empty, echoing house fragrant with Sherwin Williams' second best, so as not to miss the moving van in case it might come early. When we got up in the morning and made ready to drive through the chilly drizzle to the Hightstown diner for breakfast, we opened the front door and almost fell over a basket full of bread and jam and orange juice and hard-boiled eggs and a thermos of hot coffee. No note. Nothing to indicate who had left it there. And for the first time, while we ate standing up in the chairless house, we were able to believe that—regardless of how desolate the place appeared—it might actually, someday, become a home.

The feeling-out process started immediately. Before we brought our children, while plumbers and electricians were still getting in each others' way in the kitchen, there was a knock on the door. A pretty blonde girl of about eight stood there, looking us in the eye.

"My name is Bunny," she said, "and I hear you have two girls, and would you tell me please how old they are?"

"Four and one-and-a-half," Louise said, taken aback. "Why don't you come in for a minute?"

"No thanks," the girl answered. "I have important things to do." And tossed her white-blonde head and biked off.

A few days later two ladies arrived, one thin, one fat, like two cartoon-strip characters. They just wanted to welcome us, they said. They also wanted to know, would we be interested in joining the Pioneer Women. We had to admit that we didn't know who the Pioneer Women were. The ladies stayed for coffee and scrutinized what we were doing in the house, missing nothing, I'm sure. They left as soon as they decently could.

Later that same day old Mr. Gerson (he seemed old even then) came to collect money to buy matzos for the poor on Pesach. We gave him his dollar and he said "thank you," and shuffled out with his serene and remote smile on his bland face.

Before the week was out, and just after we had brought the

children to their new and strange home, Yetta showed up. She wanted to know if we would care to join the shul. We had no idea who she was, nor that she was a member of an influential clan. To us she was simply a pale, intense woman with graying hair and no flesh on her bones. (She still had her own hair color then; it wasn't until a good many years later that she appeared suddenly as a redhead, startling everybody at the store.)

Now, Yetta has never been shy: she came right out with the question that must have been on everyone's mind.

"Honey, are you Jewish?"

"Yes, but . . ."

"Both of you or mixed?"

"Both of us. But . . ."

"Orthodox?"

"Both our families were reformed."

"Oh."

She said it as though there were something the matter with us that was sad but not entirely our fault.

"Our shul is orthodox. But if you want to come . . ."

The woman made us feel embarrassed, we didn't quite know for what. We declined.

Yetta wasn't bothered at all. She was broad-minded, she said. Live and let live, she said, nibbling store-bought cookies.

Our two little girls had been peeking around the edge of the living room door. They wouldn't come out, though we called them. Yetta decided to give us a lecture on child-rearing. It went something like this:

"When I was a child, honey, and your parents said come, it didn't mean stay. If your mother said go to Hebrew school at four o'clock, you'd better go to Hebrew school at four o'clock, because otherwise your head would go through the wall. You didn't disobey your father or mother. Your father was like God. That's the way it was. I was raised in the old-fashioned way."

We didn't realize, of course, that henceforth, with the fundamentalist group, we were going to have two counts against us: we were Jewish, but not orthodox, and we didn't raise our kids right. It was really three counts, come to think of it: we were friends of

84

the Shahns and who knows who else; probably we were the kind who would have voted for Henry Wallace.

As the months went by and spring passed into summer, we began to put together what might be called a preliminary image of the town. At that time new residents were not as commonplace as they have since become. We were as novel to the town as the town was to us. People poured in and out of our house; it seemed to us that our house was becoming a sluice for people. Some of them knocked, and some didn't bother. And all of them gave us advice and talked about this infinitesimal community and its minuscule affairs, its history and its issues, with a passionate involvement that astonished us. All except one: Mr. Blumstein, who raised a little flock of chickens in his back yard down the street, and who brought us a paper bag of eggs once a week. He never spoke about the town at all. He wanted to talk about nothing except astronomy. Other people told us that he had come to the Homesteads in its early days as a veteran of another co-operative venture that had failed somewhere out West. The second failure here may have been too much for him: now he allowed himself to become active in local business only in the *Kultur Abend,* the cultural club which invited speakers for the edification of a shrinking public, and at budget time, when he objected strenuously to any expenditure whatever. He was old and had finished with his working life. His wife had died of cancer. Now all he wanted was to discourse upon the mystery of the stars: I guess he'd given up on this planet.

As for the rest of them—in our whole lives we'd never run into such an orgy of total recall and interpretation and warnings and helpful hints, offered with the very best intentions (even the poison), all contradictory and long, and continuing into the small hours until we were overwhelmed. It was so completely unexpected. There seemed to be no end of coffee cups to wash. In this village where there was obviously nothing to do, we found it hard to get to sleep. We'd never had such an active night life. Nobody ever went home before midnight, and some stayed a lot later. We would never have thought that there would be so much to talk about in so small a place. Of course, nobody agreed on anything with anybody, except maybe, the notion that Roosevelt, New Jersey, was unlike any other town and that this difference was important.

One day, with the summer gone and autumn in the air and the leaves, I looked at my wife in a moment when we were alone.

"You know what?" I said, really quite astonished by the idea. "We left one island and landed on another."

And that was true enough, as far as it went.

9

All the talk in our living room and in other people's
living rooms had left my mind littered with details out of se-
quence. Through them I could make out the history of the town
as no more than a broken line.

Oh, I learned about Benjamin Brown. I'd heard a number of
versions of who he was and what he did and how he died. Especially how he died. His death, after all, was no small-town death.
It had size, it had drama, particularly his disoriented wandering,
with his mind struck dumb, just before the end. It had grandeur
enough to dwarf any of the pettinesses (which over the long run
so few were able to resist, but which, I suspect, nearly all were
secretly ashamed of). The twentieth-century entrepreneur visited
personally—like Job, almost—by timeless God: from the way
people talked about it, I could sense a quality of myth. Some of
them seemed to take no little satisfaction in it.

By the time we arrived, there were no visible traces of
Brown's dream except the town itself and the factory building
which then housed a highly automated manufacture of buttons; it
gave no work to speak of to anyone in town. All the co-ops were
dead. But still, in some way I couldn't quite comprehend, something remained—a presence I couldn't put a name to. Regardless
of suspicions and divisions and slanders, some cohesive force
caused people to close protectively around any citizen in trouble

and made them behave more like members of a family than residents who had been thrown together in a small town by the accidents of life.

Take the case of Vilma, the widow of Erich Morvay, a refugee who had bought the store after the co-op folded and who had died suddenly not long before we came. Vilma was a slight, frail woman with the voice of a timid bird. When, from one day to the other, she found herself without a husband and with two children to raise, she simply couldn't face the buying and selling and all the haggling customers who had to be dealt with in the shaky, understaffed business. Erich had always taken care of that until he keeled over on a tennis court and left her stranded.

Well, the store didn't have to close. All sorts of unlikely people appeared, as though it were the most natural thing in the world for a well-known documentary photographer to drive twenty miles to Trenton to buy vegetables or a young professional to throw up his job and start clerking in a grocery.

"I had never worked in a store in my life," Milton told me. "A group of people who had known Erich, who had played tennis with him and had been to his house, called a sort of meeting in a home, saying: how will we do it? Somebody had to be there. I was the most available. So I offered to work in the store."

Just like that. And not for a couple of weeks, to help out. For six months, no less.

Milton was still there when we went to the store for the first time. We found a converted wooden construction shack, dark and not very appetizing, which went back to the time, nearly twenty years earlier, when the town had been built. It was dingy, that was the word for it. It was also cheerful and friendly; nobody seemed to mind the cold draft from the door that banged every time a customer went in or out. There was a chatter of talk; everybody knew everybody else: Buxbaum behind his counter, ready for action, Milton in the meat corner, and somebody—I don't remember who—at the cash register. Milton gives the picture better than I can:

"People used to come into the store and ask for chopped meat. I had to learn to use the band saw which terrified me. I also

88

learned to grind meat. The myth with the ladies was that you should have neck meat because it had more blood and made the chopped meat good. After a while I began to invent neck meat. We used to say: 'Let's draw a picture of the ideal cow.' And it would look like a giraffe. . . . It disturbed me that I didn't know more about how an animal was put together and which were the good parts, and how to make the cuts. It's a skill I didn't have. I couldn't even read a meat chart.

"The funny thing is that any time any human being appears behind a meat counter . . . well, you just don't realize how women who have been cooking for forty years—how little they really know. If you're at the butcher counter, you can't convince them that you know nothing. So they would start asking me how to prepare this cut of meat. They knew I wasn't a butcher, but they'd ask me anyway. I tried to tell them how little I knew, but after a while, in self-defense, I'd tell them how to handle it. Nobody died, but a few ladies said it was tough after they cooked it my way. . . .

"In retrospect the ladies were fun. At the time they were a pain in the ass. I wasn't only the butcher, you know, I worked where I was needed. One day Mrs. Rappaport walked into the store holding a pot of milk which she had boiled. And quite naturally after boiling the milk had formed a skin. And she stuck it under my nose, saying: 'Look, you sold me bad milk!' And she would not listen to any reason at all why it had formed a skin. Really, a daily diet of Mrs. Rappaport and her peers became a bit much. . . .

"But that was not the reason I finally had to leave. It was so discouraging to face what a tiny amount the store made. I felt guilty to take any money out of it. But here I was, the only one in the family working and I had to take something. . . . Besides, I wasn't giving any kind of skilled support to the store. I was a body. I suppose I left because it seemed unfair to Vilma if I stayed. . . ."

Shorlty afterwards Murray Greenbaum bought the store, lock, stock and pickle barrel. He ran it for a while until it burned one night, all the way to the ground. And then he built his new store, the one we have at present, which doesn't look in the least like a migrant workers' barracks, but abounds in neon and stainless steel and frozen food compartments; and this, I suppose, is progress. But as far as we were concerned, we had developed an affection for the old place, partly because of the story attached to it, and partly, I hate to admit, because it seemed picturesque.

Not that I knew it, you understand. But—well, how could I be expected to grasp, all of a sudden, what was real to an Eastern European garment worker of orthodox Jewish persuasion? Where was I supposed to get the equipment to read him? It might have been easier if I had been a Presbyterian or a Catholic. My roots were too close, and yet too alien. I soon found myself suspended in a sort of limbo, neither in nor out.

At least I didn't turn out black. At the time I wasn't conscious that some of our more frightened solid citizens were worried about this before they had a chance to look me over.

Granted, I should have realized that a ghetto-on-purpose (and what else should Benjamin Brown's dream colony be called?) couldn't help but share some of the paranoias characteristic of all ghettos. There had to be a certain amount of suspicion and fear of the outside and the outsider; and simultaneously there had to be the contradictory drive for safety, for becoming invisible by merging, by donning the garments of the enemy. But then I had nothing in me to make me ready for staunch union men and women scared witless because a black family might move in and decrease the value of their little "propity." I never thought about it. It didn't occur to me how strong the antibodies must be in an individual to render him immune to a disease infecting the whole country.

Where we had just come from skin color was a minor factor in determining where a man was fitted. It would be fair to say that when we first arrived we were as close to being colorblind as it was possible for white Americans to be. Even so we couldn't help noticing that the only dark people we ever got to see—the driver of the garbage truck and a small number of women who did the dirty work in the more affluent households—were living out of town, as often as not in converted chicken coops.

We saw it, but it didn't really penetrate until one very bad winter. I don't recall whether it was the first or the second or the third. It was colder than usual, that I remember, and the ice was thicker and lasted longer; and one day a black man was found frozen to death in his shack. It may have happened within our borough limits or just outside: in either case it was too close to our lives.

And a shiver passed through the town, and there was more than the normal gabble of talk at the store, and some pity expressed and some vague guilt unspoken.

Maybe we should have done something. But what? No human being ought to live or die like that.

But then it was put aside, as death is put aside.

"He was a drunk," people said. "If he'd have been sober it wouldn't have happened."

As if that excused it.

And we, in our family, had to learn to see color again, as it was dividing this country and as it was getting ready to tear the whole society apart, in spite of the Supreme Court decision, which was supposed to fix everything up.

Anyway, we did have one colored teacher in our school. (You could still use the word then; brown people hadn't yet started insisting that they were black.) She was a sweet, bewildered and very Christian girl, this teacher, and she couldn't quite figure out where she belonged in a lily-white community full of Jews. Our elected Board of Education had hired her, which went to show how up-to-date our town was. Not many small schools in the area had a colored teacher to point to.

It wasn't our fault if no colored family had chosen to live in town, was it? Nothing we could do about it, was there? Of course there was a handful of troublemakers who said that we ought to do something about it.

And then, without telling anybody beforehand, one of these—who happened to be moving away for business reasons—had the gall to dig up a colored family from God only knew where and to try renting his house to them.

And that was when the venom spilled out. All the hidden bile and the suspicion of outsiders in general, plus the terror of blacks sucked out of the very air of the vast prejudice called New Jersey, plus the fables and horror stories told about lazy, shiftless, immoral niggers and how they preferred to live in squalor and how they cut each other with razors, and anyone who happened to get in their way as well—all this folklore came out from under the bland and taken-for-granted liberality and was suddenly present in full public view, like a small, shiny, purulent boil which had appeared overnight on a lovely face that up to then had seemed free of blemishes to everybody.

A very small, a pathetic little boil, if such a thing can be imagined. I have never known the exact number of visitors who showed up that evening when the news leaked out, to wheedle and cajole and plead with the owner of the house and to warn and finally to threaten: maybe five or six. They were, I suspect, only the most hysterical of many more well-hidden bigots we had in this wonderful town of ours and never found out about before. But then, maybe I exaggerate. I was so furious about this treason to what the town was supposed to stand for that I can still taste my anger of fifteen years ago, when I happen to think back to that day.

Worst of all, these protectors of the purity of our wonderful town were no pip-squeaks of recent arrivals: among them were, I have been assured, pillars of the community, founding members from the co-op and depression days who must have learned when they were younger what prejudice felt like on their own souls and bodies. And yet there it was (quite possibly astonishing to themselves), the willingness to step on another human being as they had once been stepped on, and the willingness to expose their obscenity in front of the appalled house owner who had—for all I know—played pinochle with them for years.

Obviously they didn't see themselves as traitors to their heritage, nor as monsters of any kind. They were being no more than responsible home owners, conservationists you might say, trying to preserve Roosevelt, New Jersey, against an outside world that was attempting to make it over in its own abominable, decaying image.

And the home owner? He was a man of principle. Besides, at that time, finding a good tenant wasn't so easy. He rented the house, as arranged.

Who knows what sort of struggle might have followed, how the forces might have lined up, each waving flags and convinced that God was on its side? It could have grown into a classic Roosevelt confrontation, if there had been time for accusations to be hurled and electoral slates to be organized and programs to be stewed over and published on mimeographed sheets distributed door-to-door by small boys on bicycles. Instead it turned out, in the words of Myron, the poetic carpenter, just another tempest in a teaspoon.

The black family moved in. Two days later they moved out. Their child, it seemed, got asthma attacks from the prevalence of mold in the corners and closets of the house.

Some of us felt cheated. We had been looking forward to demonstrating to that Negro family how different we were from the inhabitants of other towns. And here we were left, with our excellent good will on our hands like an undelivered present. What were we going to do with it?

The fact was that there was little we could do, what with the reluctance of nearby banks to grant mortgages on Roosevelt houses without exorbitant down payments to anyone at all, and certainly to any applicant suffering from darkening of the skin. There was nothing we could do, no matter what handsprings we performed, to bring in a black family with the will and the money to be first in an all-white community. It took a freak event of nature to deliver an appropriately qualified family.

This time the town showed its generous side, which was always astonishing, since it made the nasty, disgusting backbiting so utterly inconceivable.

The event occurred in the spring of '63, when the woods caught fire in Jackson Township. Before the last of the scrub pines had burned to black stumps, big sections of three counties had gone up in smoke from a nearby crossroads to the Atlantic thirty miles away. Nothing could stop the racing flames, not the fire companies from the big cities, and even less our dozen volunteers buzzing importantly in and out of town with their ridiculous little tank truck. But it must have given them a cherished, if temporary dignity to come back blackened and exhausted to the ordinariness of their prosaic lives: it wasn't often that a rural New Jerseyite could get a sense of his own personal valor so close to home.

For nearly a week the air we breathed stank of burning, and our daylight was turned yellow-brown. But we felt safe: the wind kept blowing southeast away from us. And, as the sky-high smoke clouds retreated, we began worrying about the many small householders who had their shacks and cabins where the fire had been centered, deep in those ruined woods. We all knew people who had been living in there.

What had happened to them? Were they alive? Were their homes gone? A group of us piled into cars and tried driving down to find them, but the roads were barricaded by police. They had enough trouble; they didn't need carfuls of gaping fire tourists who might get caught in the unpredictable blaze and need rescuing themselves.

That evening we were sitting around with friends in the living room, talking about fires and how they happened every twenty years or so, and how people always forgot and put their houses in the woods just the same. And there was a knock on the door and Grete Ulrich, the kindergarten teacher from our school, stood there with a knot of people behind her and she said: "Our house has just burned to the ground."

She said it matter-of-factly, as she might tell us where she had bought the winter coat she was wearing.

We asked her in and found chairs for her and her shrunken apologetic husband and their mumbling, retarded boy who lived in his own world and was clutching something to him—I don't remember what—as if his whole future happiness depended on it; and half a dozen people we didn't know, a mother with a flock of kids, Polish they were, I think.

Louise made pots of coffee and cut all the bread in the house and brought in milk and jam and butter and whatnot, the best we could do without notice.

And Grete Ulrich began telling us what had happened and

what it was like in a forest fire. She was a middle-aged woman, short and broad, and she spoke with a pronounced German accent. Clearly she was the spokesman for this bedraggled group, who sat there, the children included, in a pale sort of silence that still had the smell of fright about it. Except Grete. You could tell that in her life the loss of a mere house by a fire that might have wiped out her and her family, was just another one of those things.

I asked for her two older children.

"Rose is away at college," she said, "and Bertold stayed behind to help some neighbors."

If she was worried about her son still back there in the middle of the fire, she didn't show it. I developed a lot of respect for Grete that evening.

"I saw the fire through the window of the beauty parlor where I went this morning, but far away, near Jacksons Mills," she told us. "And I said to the lady of the beauty parlor: 'If it comes close you have my invitation to our house.' I thought we were safe.

"But when I left the beauty parlor, I had to make a big detour because there was fire all along the highway.

"I said to my husband: 'Why don't we begin to put some of our things in the car?'

"He said: 'The fire is down by Jacksons Mills. It has nothing to do with us.' And he busied himself with other things.

"In the early afternoon a friend called up and she said: 'Why don't you start packing up? the fire's at Holmeson, and I don't trust it.'

"And, sure enough, the fire came. It came swiftly. So fast that, before we looked around, the grass all around our house was burning. And we began to pack up.

"The police and the fire company people came and said: 'You people better get out of here. Your house has woods on three sides, and it's all by itself, and it's too dangerous a situation, we might all not be able to get out of here.' And we got out. We collected our most important papers and our little brown dog, and we got out."

My wife and I made a few phone calls, and that was all it

took to organize help. The school was opened for the night and mattresses and pillows and blankets appeared, and a big dinner was prepared at somebody's house. This was a thing the town understood: a family in trouble, and a Jewish family at that, even if they were Germans and not religious. The Poles they had in tow were just a little extra work, they didn't count one way or the other.

The next morning Grete's son Bertold came with the father of the Polish family who all went off to some relatives. In the meantime a local family moved temporarily out of their home and turned it over to Grete to use while the real estate man found a place for her and her people. It all went like clockwork. Grete didn't lose a day at school. But she had to admit that, when it came time to go home after work, it felt strange to have no home to go to.

Since there was no house in town available just then, the real-estate-nik had to rent a very small one on a nearby farm. And before the week was out, people carried in tables and chairs and a big old sofa and beds and cupboards and pots and pans and dishes and everything they could think of to furnish an empty house. There was so much stuff that there wasn't room for all of it. Grete had to make up a truckload of what she didn't need and send it to others burned out in the fire.

The rescue operation was carried out without show, without organization really, between friends, you could say. People gave what they could dig up, and, in some cases, what they couldn't easily spare. A family of German Jewish refugees burned out of their home—it rang all kinds of bells. Ever since Grete was hired as a teacher we had been building myths about her and her husband and especially the retarded boy. We were sure that her husband had been crippled in a concentration camp and that there had to be a connection between the boy's condition and Nazi brutality. None of us ever asked: you didn't ask about a thing like that. And besides, it might not be true, which would have been a shame. Our need for a drama congenial to our built-in preconceptions made the facts irrelevant. By the time the fire burned her home, Grete and her family had become a symbol. Besides, they depended on us now, and we were grateful to them for that dependence. It brought us together just as effectively as more difficult and more alien requirements upon us could tear us apart. And for a long while after the fire we liked one another here in Roosevelt. Even people who hadn't been able to stand each other for years submerged their little detestations—they didn't give them up, of course; that would have been too much to ask. But because of Grete and her fire, for a while at least, we were able to like ourselves.

Probably because of this good feeling (what you might call one of our periods of détente), nobody in town could assemble sufficient hate to raise objections when a neighbor of Grete's from Jackson Township, a Negro, and his wife and children quietly rented one of our houses. He was a very circumspect man who did everything quietly. And he was exceptionally qualified: everyone had to agree to that. He worked at the RCA space center in some engineering capacity, and, what was more glamorous, he worked on space satellites. On weekends he was a minister of a colored church in Lakewood. It was, practically, an unbeatable combination: an upright Negro who formed his ambitions strictly according to white standards and who united in his activities God, Country and the Space Program. Bob Monroe had no trouble at all. Unless you count the time when somebody put sugar in his gas tank and another night when some damned fool cut up a batch of undershirts his wife had left hanging on the line. Bob didn't complain. He had the good taste to put down both acts to the pranks of children. . . .

To this day I don't know how Bob Monroe saw his place in this self-enclosed village where the apocalyptic terrors of the time were cut down to human size. It must have been comforting, I imagine, to be left alone but safe, since, once he had settled in, even the dirty little cranks stopped bothering about him.

It was harder, I am sure, to adjust to us, who thought of ourselves as the actively enlightened. We forced invitations down his throat, we fell over ourselves trying to make him feel at home. But none of us were engineers or ministers of God: there was so damned little we could talk about. Bob and his young, coffee-colored wife would sit stiffly in our functional chairs, while the pauses got longer and longer and the cookies were nibbled in thickening silence.

Whatever he may have thought of us, Bob stayed. After a year or so he had Myron build him a house with great, thick walls strong enough for a bomb shelter, on the outer edge of town. It in no way resembled the boxes we were living in and had come to take for granted. It turned out a sort of split-level fortress with all modern conveniences and wall-to-wall carpeting.

As soon as Bob had lived with us for the two mandatory years, we inveigled him to run for the Board of Education. We were proud that he was elected with a majority that couldn't have been much greater if he had been white and Jewish. But for poor Bob his tenure on the Board became, I think, a subtle form of torture. He was bewildered by the frequency of the interminable meetings with their in-fighting over policies and personalities. He was frankly bored to death by the idiotic complexities involved in running a tiny school dwarfed further by its huge mural full of oversized figures only two of which were black. He resigned before his term was over.

For those of us who had nagged him into this fiasco, Bob was a disappointment. The man had the nerve to remain himself instead of living up to our expectations of what he ought to be. Something snapped, or perhaps it simply died off. And now we greet each other casually at the post office (which is the only place we ever see him) and we ask after his wife and children, and we tend not to remember that he was the first, the Negro who had the guts to face us when he had no inkling who we were.

Other families of his race have followed Bob into town. Some stayed, some left after a while. Nobody makes a fuss about them anymore, not even when there is a white woman married to a black man. Times have changed and so has the outward form of prejudice. Even the real estate man no longer hesitates to show a house for rent or sale to respectable clients with black faces. You know the old saying: some of my best friends are . . .

But there have never been more than three or four black families at any one time. They just don't seem to come here. Maybe, by now, buying a house and living in our ex-proletarian utopia has become too expensive for any except the most solvent in the newly self-conscious and most depressed group on the American scene. Or maybe they prefer going to where the action is instead of a place where nothing ever happens and where, no matter how loud a man cries out, he won't be heard beyond the borough limits.

10

Look back to the fifties: you might think that by then everyone in Roosevelt should have understood how irrevocably the whole idea of the town was becoming obsolete. Who cared about co-ops in the consumer society? And as to a chicken in every pot, it sounded like a ridiculously modest ambition in the middle of a rampaging prosperity without parallel in the history of the planet. Nobody wanted to be reminded of the depression: it was a bad dream, and the less said about it the better.

But to the old settlers the depression remained the environment of their glory. They couldn't let go of it and not lose touch with the core of their lives.

A lot of them doggedly kept on going to work every day, as they had gone as far back as they could remember, in any handy garment shop within driving distance. They had little trouble finding jobs; they were experts at their trade. They made arrangements with some driver heading in the same general direction (paying their share of gas and oil and tolls, if any) and if their transportation failed, they planted themselves at the hitching corner, and the weather be damned. They didn't thumb. They just stood there, demanding to be picked up by simply existing; not as a favor, but as a right. It was as though they knew that they had been part of a harder, more clear-eyed past and had earned a firm claim on the flimsy present.

Quite a few were baffled by their own younger generation, not angry, since they were helpless against family love, but a little embarrassed that they should have brought forth such delicate offspring.

"What makes it that they are always sick?" Goldie wondered out loud to me. "I remember Russia. I was raised and married in Russia. It was bitter there, especially for Jewish people. . . . When we came to New York in 1926 we both went to work. And it was nice. We had water in the kitchen. I was so happy to see that. I could take a bath in the kitchen. . . . But the young people today—the more they have, nice homes, cars, schools—they're always complaining, always sick. . . ."

She shook her head at me, her great eyes troubled under their painted brows.

Goldie's children—college-bred, middle-aged, married, bright and therefore dazed in their undecipherable time, are awed by her strength. The whole community seems to accept the old settlers at their own valuation. Even the newcomers to whom the story of the town is no more than a collection of romantic, picturesque anecdotes. The homesteaders are given the respect (a slightly amused respect, perhaps, in some cases) equivalent to an affectionate worship of surviving ancestors.

On the Fourth of July a handful of leftover pioneers are part of the parade, riding through town in a hired or borrowed white Cadillac convertible. The parade watchers grin at them in a friendly way. Some wave and call out. But nobody laughs.

When did these durable and cranky veterans first get to feel that their town was leaving them? I'm not the one to say. By the time we arrived, it looked, on the contrary, as if the community were going to age into the ground, leaning on canes, all at once. (The illusion could be traced back to the very beginning, I suppose, to the Senior Selection Specialist who had to find heads of families with acceptable references as stable citizens and competent machine operators. A man had to have long years on his back before he would be able to meet those requirements. Youngsters wouldn't do, although they might well have been better suited to the rigors of muddy resettlement in a government project with utopian overtones. As it turned out, most of them were close to forty when they came; which meant that a quarter of a century later nearly the whole group was hobbling toward retirement four abreast, you might say, in formation.)

But there had to be a few cynics, I should think, with the courage of their pessimism. Privately at least they must have realized that the day was coming when their children and the friends they could attract were not going to be enough to fill up the houses that were emptying so relentlessly; and that it was only a matter of some years before their town was taken over by twentieth-century carpetbaggers who didn't give much of a damn for socialist idealism or for Jewishness, for that matter.

The evidence was there, if you weren't afraid to look at it. The traditional Jewish organizations that had once dominated the life of the town were still around, the *Farband,* the IWO, the *Workmens' Circle;* but they were ailing. The *Kultur Abend* was losing out to movies as far away as Trenton, even though most of the lectures were now in English; often not more than a score of listeners could be induced to attend, and these were generally old folk who didn't see so well anymore and didn't trust themselves to drive at night. Only the Zionist *Pioneer Women* and the *Sisterhood* of the Shul still flourished, and they had to fight each other for members and money, since there didn't seem to be enough of either to go around. They could be pretty aggressive about it. The *Pioneer Women* insisted that every loose penny belonged by rights to the Israelis; the *sisterhood* was determined to build a beautiful new synagogue. "What kind of a Jew are you?" they had a way of asking, and you had better have an answer ready.

Yetta was in the middle of the struggle, as she tended to be in the middle of any town argument. On the shul side, this time.

"If we finally got a building," she explains, "you've got my father to thank for that. My father insisted that they should buy the two lots from the government. They decided where it was going to be because the spot was pretty and there were lots of pines there. We were running affairs. We used to carry the dishes from the construction shack that had been our synagogue all those years to the Hightstown synagogue and have banquets in their little basement there to raise money for here. We'd run different affairs and raffles. And when we had enough money,

then we got the mortgage. What we did first was make a foundation. And the sides came up next and then the roof came on. All
piece by piece. We got a lot of donations, and then we got the big
farmers from around here. And all the business people from
Hightstown donated, the big dairies and people like that. Little by
little we built it. We got the cheapest contractors who made the
biggest mistakes, and let me tell you, we have more leaks than
anybody you know. But it's our building, and we'll work it
out. . . ."

The new shul was finished in the middle fifties, very modernistic, concrete and glass, with big windows made of blue and
white panes in the shape of a pattern of stars of David and, on the
inside, social rooms and a kitchen for catered affairs and rest
rooms as good as any in a Texaco gas station. I remember when it
was dedicated. It was a big victory for the pious and those who
weren't so pious but wanted to look as if they were. It had been a
tremendous job to get the money together and to get the whole
enterprise organized, even though a lot of the rest of us may think
the place is something of an eyesore. Consider what it must have
meant to slug all those merchants into contributing and, maybe
hardest of all, to squeeze the local people into giving. The *sisterhood* had reason to be proud. It also has reasons to be worried
because paying for the upkeep and meeting the mortgage payments is no small burden on a shrinking congregation.

"There's only a handful of us now," Yetta goes on. "And it's
really a shame because there are still many Jewish families here.
Whether a family is mixed or not is none of our business, but still
the synagogue is something that belongs to the community and
people should really contribute to keep it going. If somebody
comes to me and asks me to buy a ticket for a church raffle, I buy
a ticket for a dollar. So, if I go to Joe Schmoe on the corner and
say our synagogue is raffling off a picture by Ben Shahn, would
you buy a ticket for a dollar, I expect no trouble. But there are
quite a few people, like the *Farband,* to them the shul is a deadly
thing. 'For the synagogue? I think that's terrible.' When they tell
me that, I die. I'll never forget one woman, right after the war, we
were selling card party tickets for a quarter. Things were pretty
rough if you were selling a ticket for a quarter—right?—and the

refreshments you were getting was practically a meal. . . . So I said: 'Would you buy a ticket, the synagogue is running a card party.' So she said: 'I'm sorry, I'm an atheist.' And I said to her: 'You'll be the first atheist Hitler will get to.' I was mad as a hornet. I mean I was so mad. I mean what else would you have said? It was only a quarter."

There was no reason to expect, of course, that all of a sudden the Jewish residents of Roosevelt, New Jersey, who had never agreed on anything before, should agree on the matter of the new shul. But there was a mellowing, no doubt about that. As Yetta puts it, when you get older, you go to God a little more: please let me have another year . . .

Herman, the opera singer, tells how it was with his father:

"My father was never very religious. Until he got to be old . . . I mean what the hell do you do in the house after you read the *Daily Forward*? Nobody to talk to except your children. So, on the Sabbath you go to the shul to see these old Jews that you got used to here in town. I can understand that. But I asked him: 'What are you doing?' I said. 'Are you returning to religion? What is this nonsense?' He said: 'No, no. But it gives me pleasure to be with them.' He was brought up a Jew, he rejected the phony part of it, and at the end of his life he returned to some of its form for his own private reasons. . . . Because my father never felt that he had sinned and that he was not at peace with God. He was in retirement and he had to have something to do. He gardened, he visited his grandchildren and he went to the shul on the Sabbath. That was his life. And he died a Jew."

The idea has grown on me since that the spurt of activity, which resulted in the building of the new synagogue after so many years of getting along in the old construction shack, might have been like the rallying of a sick man before the crisis. It's only an idea, and I have no way of proving it. I don't imagine for a moment that the ladies of the *sisterhood* were aware of what was driving them; that it could be the old terror of being drowned in a flood of strangers; the old fear of the pogrom, the old suspicion of the Gentile. Maybe they sensed that their whole culture was in peril, not immediately, but in the long run, in this very enclave where until then they had felt protected.

I could be all wrong. It was the age of Sputnik and of ominous stirrings in America and in the world. Different observers might draw very different conclusions about the nature of the anxieties moving people at that time, not just in this one remote little town with its habit of thinking itself unique.

The new shul isn't new anymore; it has become part of the landscape. It is still the only religious institution in town. Only on the high holidays, the Jewish New Year, the Day of Atonement and in the spring on Passover can you get some of the flavor of what the community used to be. On those days the businessmen and doctors and scientists and lawyers come back from out-of-town with their elegant wives and children to join the old folks in rites that may not mean much to them anymore except, perhaps, as an affirmation of loyalties which it might bother them to deny entirely. On those days the shul fills up and so does the street. Driving is out; everybody walks. During the service friends who haven't seen each other for months come out for a breath of air and to talk, with their white prayer shawls casually draped over their Hart, Schaffner and Marx's. In the morning on the way to the shul and in the evening on the way home streams of people (looking a little self-conscious as people will in their go-to-meeting best) dribble along the street, taking up the whole width. A car would have a hard time getting through, it would have to honk, and that would be wrong. So on those days, I, for one, avoid the block where the shul stands. I prefer to take the long way around to the dirty looks I would get as a Jew in a car and the sorrow which always comes over me when I have to witness the fading-out of something that was valid just a while ago and is now being quietly phased out.

11

When you look back on a time of change, you are apt to think first of the old people, and how hard it must have been for them. But here, when the town changed from a workers' town with a rooted European Jewish way of seeing life to an American middle-class town that was being rolled over by God's country on six-plys—why, it was hard on the children too, just as hard as for the grownups.

The ghetto may look confining from the outside; but growing up in it, you feel it's made to understand you and to being understood by you. You have this magic circle around you, and magic circles are very real to children. Every game of catch has its home base.

Well, there used to be a pretty girl in town—she's moved away now to California, and she comes back only on short visits—who was brought up within this particular magic circle. She isn't much of a talker, but if she gets started on what her childhood was like, she can't stop. It hounds her, I think, this remembered childhood, especially when she's away; but when she comes back to visit and has to face the smallness of living here and the bigness of the boredom that sits over it like a lid, it drives her out of her mind. And before long she's got to flee to her commune in San Francisco.

"I've sort of broken my ties to Roosevelt," Carol says. "It was a big part of my life, but it's over, you know. It kind of saddens me the way Roosevelt is separating or something. You know, there's just not that old, old, deep family love that there used to be. . . . I mean, God, I remember, like the old store, Erich Morvay had it, and there used to be a soda fountain there, and Vilma and, I guess, her mother used to make hot lunches for the kids. All of us whose parents were working used to eat lunch at the store. It was just like eating home, all the food homemade. . . . You know, Roosevelt became sort of like your mother's womb. When I think back to the time I was about ten years old, it was really a good place. I had a lot of friends when I was little, and we did a lot of fun things, like playing in the woods, you know, and building huts, and parties and picnics at Washington's Crossing on Sundays. . . ."

I wonder if Carol hasn't constructed that pastel-colored childhood for herself because she needs it to stand on if she's going to stand at all. She's had a pretty rough time since then, a couple of failed marriages, not to mention assorted troubles she had before. She seems to find it difficult to fit in anywhere. She's stuck with a baby girl now, who has inherited her fine dark eyes, but who doesn't make floating around any easier.

"Roosevelt's changed a lot from the time when I was really young," she explains. "I can look at people that we used to do things with, and, like, all of a sudden they've gotten tired. It used to be—whenever they saw you, they used to stop and be friendly and talk to you, you know. Now it's hello and good-bye. I think it's just the difference in the way you look at a town when you're little. . . . Like it was just hard to get out of Roosevelt. Maybe you weren't so sure you wanted to get out in the big world. You know, you've grown up in this little town that's full of intellectual people and this and that, and you sort of think that's the way life is. But there's a lot of shit that goes on in life, maybe a lot of bad shit; but going through it means something. I've learned a lot, having these things put in front of me: you know, this is what you want and this is what you don't want. . . ."

What did Carol learn? I doubt that she knows. Not so that

she can put her finger on it at least, since pinpointing seems to be as foreign to her as precision to her speaking. In this, I suppose, she's a member of that numberless kin who grew up with the impermanence of the species hung around their necks and who have been blindly seeking home ever since. And the place where her growing up happened, she's finding out, won't do anymore.

Roosevelt won't do anymore for Carol because it's not only that the people who surrounded her sacred childhood are growing old and introverted; it's that the backwash of the horrendous, sickly, worldwide bitter flood has seeped into that sweet, remembered magic circle and spoiled it. She would be outraged, I'm sure, if anyone were to suggest that she, pretty little Carol with the big eyes, had her part in that alteration; that her personal, piddling, snot-nosed rebellion from the time she was a high school kid in Hightstown—her little revolution by parental permission—was one small dig added to a lot of others, that helped erode whatever had kept her home place inviolate. It could even be—it's not unreasonable to suppose—that the people who now say just hello and good-bye have in fact remained more what they always were than she can afford to see: that in truth it's she who has put on a different skin, and that maybe they can't know her any longer as they used to know her; that they simply don't know how to speak to her.

I'm not blaming Carol; I wouldn't think of it. She is what she is, and she has to live with it and chew on it and try to build a world out of it that she can tolerate. So she's a tame bird flying wild, one of millions; and that is sad to watch since the wings are clipped to start with. She didn't invent the impotent freedoms, nor the speed and the acid and the pot to give them an appearance of validity. She didn't bring into town either the revolt of estrangement nor the medicaments that go to make it plausible. Somebody had to, I guess, but it makes no difference who it was anymore than it matters who carries any wide contagion: it can't be avoided, it's everywhere like the air.

It does count that the community of Roosevelt stands in one of a union of states which has lost its way so badly it has finally scared itself till the old can't talk to the middle-aged and a lot of the kids can't talk at all: they struggle and they mumble around an idea as if it were a biting snake. And that is our time, our miserable, disgusting time, and it spills over us here in our patch of separateness; and the old socialists become the establishment and the people who go to work every day become the squares and one day, to nobody's surprise, the state police surround a house with a bunch of kids in it and arrest them for possession.

And everybody feels bad and some are angry and some shrug: but they all talk. Talk and talk. And just about then Carol arrives on one of her visits from California.

"I don't know, people get so wrapped up in this town," Carol says. "Like two people sitting in the living room discussing something that happened at the post office. Or the latest bust. Just like the first night when I got home. First thing I walked in, my mother said to me: 'Did you hear about the bust?' And I said: 'Yeah, I heard about it.' And she said: 'Well—what do you know about it?' I said: 'Mommy, I don't know anything about it.' And I walked into the living room, my father's asleep on the couch, and he wakes up and he says: 'Do you know anything about this bust?' I said: 'Jesus Christ, I don't even live here. . . .'

"You know, I just get tired of all the crap, everybody knows what you're doing. That first day I got home I had to go down to the store and Ursula is there, and she has a kind of snide hello for me. And I just decide I'm not going to let any of this get me down, and I just joyfully said: 'Hi, Ursula, how are you?'

"I think for the first time, you know, like I can really stand back and look at people here instead of getting involved with them. Just like that other night with Paula screaming about the school at the Morgensterns' house: I just sort of sat there and laughed at the whole thing. Like before that, I would probably have gotten all excited about hearing all the gossip, you know the Board of Education, the typical hassle that Roosevelt has every year, and who is doing what. But all of a sudden it was like I was just sitting there watching a play going on, and I didn't care; and it felt good. . . . When I think of when I was married to Charlie and we were living in Roosevelt, how much time we spent talking about other people in town! George Buxbaum and I were rapping about it the other night. I was over there till really late and I said: 'Jesus, George, what do people really do in Roosevelt?' You know, I'm not talking about people like my parents, I'm talking about, like, our own generation. And he said: 'Well, why do you think I'm just sitting here, watching television? . . .'"

So Carol is at last freeing herself from the tight hold of the littleness that, up to now, was strong enough to reach across three thousand miles and disrupt her sleep in California. Or so she says. I wouldn't want to estimate how much of her confusion should be charged to the town and the period when she came of age in it. She has an older sister who was always the talented one, the one who made the honor society, the one who got the ballet lessons: that sister still lives here, successful as always, a mother and a wife and quietly cool. That's what it looks like, anyway, from the street: but who knows what goes on behind the closed doors? I could write about her and I could venture all kinds of conjectures as to the inner drives that caused her and the gifted local boy she married to amass an incredible collection of nineteenth-century leftovers—apple corers, cash registers, old guitars, cookie forms, carpenter's tools and quite inconceivable assorted junk—until their house can't hold it. She weaves, beautifully, meticulously, from the spinning of the thread up, and colors her lovely fabrics with dyes cooked up according to forgotten recipes in some long-out-of-print manual for housewives. It's a revolt too, I guess, against shoddiness and mass production, and the supermarket: but it bothers nobody, it's so unobtrusive and private and kept silenced within the walls of the house. And so nobody gossips about her; her alienation is no taunt to anyone; and that in itself is a kind of success, or at least it must look that way to Carol, who can't keep her turmoil quiet, who must flail and lash out.

"You know, my sister has always done really well," Carol says. "When I got to high school everybody was surprised that I wasn't getting really good grades like she did before me. You know, I can't get into all this psychology, because I really don't know. I just think that I was rebelling against everything she did, you know, sort of trying to do the opposite, until I just sort of made that my way of life."

Now, perhaps, Carol can make friends with her sister. She tells me that the two of them can talk to each other as they never could before.

How well she can talk to her parents is a question they certainly could not answer. But then how well does anybody? They are grand people, understanding, warm, tolerant to a fault. He's a print-maker and a teacher and an artist into his very bones; she a Midwesterner who came East full of the idealism Americans used to take for granted as part of their heritage: and together they fought the world. By now the weariness is showing, the juice is drained: and they stand before their angry child, offering themselves, but not able to help much. At least she does come home once in a while, and that is something: they have learned to be grateful for splinters of love even if they hurt.

Carol knows this, and it bothers her.

"I was just having a morbid review the other day," she tells. "I was lying in the living room, and I was looking at all the pictures and all the parents' shit, you know. And I said to myself, one day my sister and I are going to inherit all this. Just what I need: a house in Roosevelt! Like, I really don't want to live here again. But I sort of wouldn't like to sell the house, because that house is my parents'.

". . . All right, the stuff in the house I can take with me, you know, and do something with it, wherever I am. But the gardens outside—like all the work my parents did outside, the ferns from all over the country planted in that garden. Those are always going to be here. . . ."

But Carol isn't, I guess. She's going to be finding her way somewhere else. It's hard to anticipate the time when your parents are going to be dead: to think about it is enough to stir up guilts you didn't know you had and bring to the surface sad feelings of compassion which may well have to do with being sloppily sorry for yourself. But the dissolution of your own magic circle has to be recognized for what it is, right now.

Sometimes on a gray day before the spring really gets going I get depressed—as who doesn't?—and I see one of the young professionals who have recently come to town in growing numbers.

He's training a pup, a purebred animal, not a mutt such as used to be common in town.

"Heel," he commands. "Sit," he orders.

How long will he be here, this young man with his long hair and beard? A year? Two years?

12

The damnedest people kept floating in and out of town.

A general staff colonel getting a fast Ph. D. at Princeton before going off to Vietnam.

A fabric designer from Brooklyn who hated his job and played country music on the banjo to ease his existential loneliness. According to the gossip he'd gotten himself a girl friend from a computerized dating service.

A blond, athletic engineer fresh out of West Germany. Even with his shirt off, bronzed from sun-bathing, he resembled the very stereotype of the *Waffen SS*. What did he want in our nest of Jews?

A paper salesman whose kids had changed school five times before he came here, and who didn't last two months before he was transferred to Ohio.

And then most startling, most strange, the mild bland-faced student of the church organ at a nearby choir school, who made no splash at all until about a year after he moved in with his shy wife and new baby: until the state police came to arrest him one day on a charge of having beaten that baby to death.

Obviously, the levees built by the founders were leaking and the new time was dribbling in, you could see the crumbling damp spots. All over the place you could see them. But somehow we kept on, day to day, as if nothing were happening.

We were too mesmerized by our nostalgias to admit that our very special town might ever be turned into another inexpensive motel for the middle-class migrants shoved about the country by twentieth-century corporate America. So the pensioners in Florida were putting their homes up for short-term rent? And the children of dead homesteaders, long prosperously settled elsewhere, were doing the same? Let the renters come and go, we thought, the town needs new blood.

We didn't wake up even when a developer threw up a couple of dozen plywood and sheet-rock ranchers less than a mile from the store. ROOSEVELT ESTATES, no less. A minuscule Levittown. Was that the shape of our future? We refused to consider it. Nobody was going to take us away from us. Even if we had to go around with our eyes shut. . . .

The fact was that many of us carried the threat inside, a persistent little discomfort that was better not closely examined.

We didn't fight about this one; there were no quarrels connected with it that I can remember. The thing went too deep. Besides, what could we do?

Well, the chance to do something came with the approach of the twenty-fifth anniversary of the founding of the community. Ben Shahn supplied the idea. He proposed that a memorial to Franklin Roosevelt should be built on the school grounds, a project that had been attempted years earlier and then abandoned for lack of funds: a small amphitheatre around a reflecting pool and a monumental bust of the late president. Only this time we were not going to try raising all the money in town; we were going outside, to anybody at all who had the same feeling as our own, and who had cash to spare.

I ought better amend that: Ben was going to go out to raise the bulk of the money. He was the only one who had the standing and the connections. It soon became obvious that the whole thing had to be Ben's show.

It couldn't help but be. Because over the years Ben had become an international figure. He was pampered with awards and honorary degrees. In his studio he had a special drawer where he tossed medals as if they were quarters. The invitations to talk and teach at universities were lying around on the edge of his worktable. He was given one-man exhibitions at home and abroad, and he was a power when he walked into a museum or a lecture hall. Celebrities and students on the make from all over the world flocked to his house to sit at the feet of the great man and to be fed by poor Bernarda, who had to whip up fancy dinners on such short notice they gave her migraines. The Ben Shahn boom, which had started out modestly years ago when a few collectors and museum directors put their money on the controversial maverick to whom little except his own truth was sacred, now burst open like a piñata at a birthday party, and everybody scrambled for a piece of it. Even the federal authority (although some sectors of it still looked upon him as politically suspect) endorsed his foreign showings, in the hope, I suppose, that maybe, maybe, some of Ben's humanism might rub off on the image of the United States. And Ben loved it. That was how it seemed, at least.

Now he could expand; now, in the evenings or on weekends, when he emerged from the trance of his work in the studio, he had no trouble anymore finding receptive listeners for his imperious legend broken down into fragments of picturesque little stories. Connoisseurs with big reputations, historians, wealthy men who brought sophisticated gifts because they thought they loved him, when in fact most of them relished the reflection of his fame upon themselves; men with ambitious projects, theatrical and ballet producers begging him to create posters, scenery and costumes for their avant-garde spectacles; writers and publishers pleading for illustrations of books or articles; all of them eager to possess any product of the miraculous hand, any doodle, and willing to pay handsomely. More than ever he was in demand on television, where his natural tendency to trip up pooh-bahs made for the kind of controversy likely to improve the ratings of culturally oriented talk shows. It was, you might say, the flowering of Ben's movie-star period, and he exulted in it. Or so it seemed.

All this while he was living in our hamlet of former tailors only recently discovered by assorted strangers in search of cheap housing. True, he spent a lot of time out of town; he went on extended trips to far places. But he belonged to us, there was no question about that. And some of the aging residents were pleased: one of our boys made it. And they may have walked a little straighter knowing that again, as in the old days, their village was not just an anonymous spot on the map. Even if, as Stella says, Ben was no figure of awe to them.

And then, of course there were others who resented his sudden rise out of their reach, who felt abused by it and diminished. Not that Ben had changed—or at least he didn't know that he had changed—toward the people at the post office in the morning. But some of them may have felt that he had, especially other artists or would-be artists, and unsure individuals who were secretly insulted because they weren't invited to those evenings at his house when the big wheels were there.

Stella analyzes their feelings pretty well:

"It was like the Arthur Miller thing," she says, "where he says at the end of *Death of a Salesman:* 'Attention must be paid, Attention must be paid.' Everybody inside himself is saying: 'Attention must be paid.' A successful man is a measure. And respect from him is a measure of you. Inside yourself you are a human being and you're suffering and struggling. Perhaps you haven't achieved. But the only thing you haven't done is achieve. In every other way you've been as human as anybody else. And when you feel that somebody has rejected you, somebody very successful, you can't say to yourself—well, that's a fair judgment."

The fact is that the whole American heritage makes success the measure, that the successful man becomes the pinnacle of the social order, and that those who frequent his house are near the top of the pyramid. And this happened with Ben, though I don't think he was conscious of it or wanted it or did anything to bring it about. And some of the resentment was pretty virulent.

Take for instance what a friend of his had to say (and he was a friend, though he could be as sharp-tongued about Ben as he was about everybody else). This college-educated man lived by manual skill because he had learned from his steelworker father that this was the only honest way to be. Since he has lived here he has started to paint, and Ben was helpful to him, and, as far as I know, he, the friend, still paints in his basement in Roosevelt Estates when he comes home after working all day at his job. He's a man of strong opinions and cutting, often shrewd judgments, and he's known all over town for his erratic, visceral eloquence.

"When you live in Roosevelt," he said to me once, "you might well make the mistake to consider him the only artist in America. You'd see his work popped up at you in the newspaper and in the post office. It's in the school. It's on a lot of people's walls. But you know, it's a big world out there and he was just one of the many figures in that world. . . . I, for one—and this is purely personal—I think it's a crime what happened to him in his later life. He was tense, he was nervous, he had no sense of ease. He didn"t enjoy himself. He seemed to be the creature captive of that fucking madness that went on every weekend around his house. If I didn't know better, I'd say that this is a young kid who's being sucked at for Hollywood or something. . . . But he had it made! He had money. Did you ever see that group of freaks that used to trot in and out of that door? Those two-dimensional horrors that used to come there? The producers and politicians and television people and stuff like that. The way they were doing that Mecca routine in there. . . . I used to say to him: 'What the hell, are you nuts? . . .' I used to go to see him, not too often, maybe every couple of months. We would talk about many things, but not much about art. And I got a very, very strange feeling about the man. It was that the man that I knew in this arrangement was almost the antithesis of the man you would meet in his living room with his friends and family. Two different orders of human being. In one place he was a human being and in the other place he was sort of an actor. In his studio he had a touch of ordinariness that you could very easily adjust to—you know, somebody you knew who was working. And he did work; he never stopped working. But in his living room you had this fantastic and almost insane type of performer, where anecdotes went on. There was a kind of stylization to the procedure. I would really do my best to avoid that social animal. A man you could very easily dislike. A man who dominated the conversation. It was always a jar. . . . Who the hell was Ben? Who was that man I saw in the house and who was that man I saw in the studio? A warm, decent human being with all the ordinary *shticklach.* A man who felt deeply and could make that kind of picture. It used to trouble the shit out of me. Because in the living room you saw some maniacal quality where the world was a world that had two cases: Ben Shahn and the rest of the world. But you knew that wasn't the whole man: because look at his pictures."

This is a big part of the answer all right: look at his pictures. Making pictures mattered to Ben more than anything; the cantankerous vanity that made it necessary for him to bathe in the approval he was getting was incidental: it was part of the same drive, I'm sure, that compelled him to make pictures, make pictures up to the very moment when he died.

The powerful personality, the need to dominate, may well have come out of a basic insecurity, as some of his psychoanalytically oriented friends and critics diagnosed it. The rhythm of his endlessly repeated stories which eventually bothered everyone who spent much time with him was part of that personality: I am sure he had some inner need to repeat and repeat with variations; he was too intelligent, too self-observant not to know he was doing it. I think he may have needed that retelling to convince himself of a continuity in him. Again: look at his pictures. He could milk a symbol, once he had evolved it, using it in dozens of pictorial combinations until it ceased to be an invention and became an integral part, like an arm or a leg, in the body of his total work.

Whatever the appearances, in spite of his many political involvements, in spite of his fierce arguments with his society and especially the direction art was taking in that society, the one thing that really mattered to Ben was the act of producing images on canvas or on a wall or on paper. That act was, I feel certain, necessary to keep intact his connection with the world. Without it he would have been marooned.

Making pictures, to a man like Ben, was more than a compulsion: it was the only way he knew to keep his sanity. A man may start to paint or write or make music because he wants to when he is young; it may begin as a lighthearted decision. As he gets older, if he keeps it up, he needs to justify his difference from the wage earners who go to daily jobs. He is almost forced into the assertion that the artist is a special sort of being, entitled to subtly special consideration from those who would otherwise be his peers. He has a historic role. As Ben often pointed out, nobody remembers the prime ministers or business leaders of ancient civilizations; only the art is left over after the mud of history has buried them.

Ben could be immensely arrogant, rude, self-centered, irritating; he could also be kind, helpful, brilliant, stimulating. His friends (and I specifically include myself) accepted his idiosyncrasies, they didn't need to forgive him anything, no matter how annoyed they were with him at times. It was all made right on the day—which came every once in a while—when he phoned and his voice was tense with a peculiar excitement and said: "Come on over, I've got something to show you." And you'd go to his house and the door to the studio stood open, and there was his latest work, still wet, propped up and he beside it, uncertain and hopeful as a child: here was a new picture, a newborn thing that had not existed before, and you didn't know what to say, you were speechless before it.

While the newness of his latest work was still upon him, before he sent it away to his gallery in New York, Ben had to have some feeling of sharing it with someone. And this, I find, is a requirement of many creative people who, if they are worth a damn, doubt themselves constantly.

As far as we were concerned, when Ben called us like that out of the blue, we knew it was a gesture of fellowship; we couldn't help feeling flattered. We didn't waste time; we dropped whatever we were doing and drove over there right away. Not just to see Ben, but to see the new picture in the same room with the man who had made it: and that to us was the real Ben Shahn, the one that mattered.

When Ben was young and slapped the proper world with his Sacco and Vanzetti series, he relished the execrations of the staid and the plaudits of the avant-garde; in his middle age and later, he had to make do with the approval of the establishment. It probably wasn't what he really would have liked, but it was better than no approval at all; and it had its rewards, comfort and money and kudos, and that may well be irresistible in the long run. It hurt him, I think, to be rejected as old hat by the up-and-coming young and their prophets. Luckily for him there were enough members of his own generation alive (and often in control of power in the art world) to convince him that his work had meaning, whenever he despaired of it. I, as a member of that generation, found much that was meaningful to me revealed in his images. And I couldn't have cared less about the dissent of the fashionable critics.

Ben was, obviously, much more than a talent with a need to have its ego diapered. He was a man of ravenous curiosity whose interests ranged from atoms to politics, from the arts and literatures of man to history and biology. He read whatever came to hand, the latest and the oldest, fiction, poetry, and the abstruse disputation of the learned. How he found time to read as much as he did (and he was no fast reader, he despised fast reading) I have never been able to figure out.

He was an intellectual, I guess; as many a pundit found out, when he got into an argument with him. Also he could laugh. His gift for finding the ridiculous in any pretense served him to keep perspective; he never lost sight of the worm of self-importance in Prometheus, though he believed fervently in the struggle toward whatever truth was currently available for exploration. (Except the space program: it bored him, he said, and he claimed that he didn't watch the thundering takeoffs on TV that had the rest of us chewing our fingernails. Maybe there was more than boredom in his resistance: I wouldn't be surprised if the whole stupendous effort, surrounded by ballyhoo, struck him as lacking in respect for the universal mystery.) Because Ben —no matter how much of freethinker he thought himself to be— was essentially religious. He was a skeptic who believed in miracle and myth. He was filled with awe by the creation—from molecule to nebula, from a stalk of wheat to a loving couple in the grass. And if you followed his thought far enough to get near its source, you were likely to come on the ancient ethic that had motivated the Jewish garment workers who migrated from the city to the wilds of New Jersey in pursuit of the will of God, equality, justice and a decent living. And this, more than anything else, I am convinced, maintained intact his bond to the community.

His frustrations in this respect were, I think, the products of his complicated ambivalence. He had no patience with the shul crowd; yet he gave them a print to sell when they were raising money. If he happened to be feeling folksy, he could be understanding and warm with our provincial burghers; but if something happened to make him angry, he could blast them as narrow, ignorant, bigoted, greedy and bitchy enough to destroy a neighbor for the fun of it. He visited with other professional artists in town; but, as one of them puts it: "He always placed himself by force into a position where he could be the father figure. He had to consume people. . . ."

Other local painters who had arrived as unknowns and gradually achieved a measure of recognition say in one way or another that Ben used to be most helpful while they were struggling, and became sarcastic and even insulting once they had established their own place in the hierarchy of art. At least they felt he was insulting, and they still bear that grudge, a lot of them do, like a hidden tumor, under their easy rhetoric of admiration, now that Ben is dead.

What he liked best was to play the part of apostle of the arts. At Christmas time he gave away dozens of serigraphs as though they were so many greeting cards: the walls of Roosevelt houses are hung with examples of his work, prints which have now become valuable, so that some of their owners are beginning to inquire for the first time about the cost of insurance.

In my opinion Ben knew exactly what he was doing to the town. He was flooding the philistines with art, he was getting them accustomed to living with it; he was converting them.

The case of Si Pinsker is as good an example as any:

"He used to always admonish me not to play the stock market," Si says. "I should buy art. Art books. He contended that the best investment was in art books. He used to tell me about friends who had invested in art and how much money they made. I didn't listen to him. I stayed in the stock market and I'm still in trouble. Just imagine if I had just bought Ben's art with all the money I put in the stock market, how much more my money would be worth now."

This was the same Si who had been a member of the Civic League at the time of its most violent attacks on Ben. He's positively tearful now. Ben knew how to disarm enemies by sticking his needle into their most vulnerable spots.

"When he used to tell me to buy art, I'd tell him I couldn't afford it. 'If you smoke,' he'd say, 'you can afford art. If you really want it, you'll find a way.' And of course it was true. . . . And I bought a few pieces from him. In the beginning he wouldn't sell art to anybody in Roosevelt; he'd either give it away or tell them to go to his gallery. And I'd say: 'I'll be goddamned if I'll go to the gallery and pay them a third higher than what I can get it for from you!' He wouldn't do it, he just wouldn't do it for years. And then, somehow, I broke through. I don't know how I did it, but finally he sold me a piece and then another piece and another piece. The last one I bought, at his insistence, I didn't have the money at the time—he made me pay five dollars a week, he wanted it that way. It got to be a pain in the ass. I'd forget, and I'd have to make out four five-dollar checks instead of one check for twenty. He was already dead and buried when I got my bank statement with the last canceled check. That was for the picture with the angel singing and playing the harp. . . ."

And there is Lou Perlmutter, the retired accountant, bull-necked, blunt, a veteran of wars and many a local skirmish, with big, knobby features in a leathery face, opinionated and forever ready for a scrap: the last man you would think of as an artist. But Ben must have discerned the poetic yearning under the belligerence. And, whatever it was he saw there stimulated Ben to have a try at this unlikely candidate.

"I used to meet him at the post office," Lou told me, "and he'd say: 'What are you doing?'

"And I'd say: 'Nothing,' see.

" 'Why?'

"I'd say: 'No ideas,' see.

"He says: 'Take a piece of wood, put it on a bench and start to cut. Work at something. Do it. The ideas will come.'

"And he was right. You take a piece of wood—that plum tree I had out there, see. I cut a piece of it off—just for something to do, see. I cut away all the soft stuff, and I discovered this is a beautiful piece of wood. But it had nothing, no shape or form. Still, if you looked at it long enough, you could see a face on one side and something else on the other side. Over a period I cut up the whole tree, see, and I got a whole series of pieces out of it. Later I made a menorah. That one I made of brass. And then I made it in wood, and then in aluminum, see. And the reason I made it in brass is that I had the brass. And the reason I made the next one in wood is I had the wood. I find my material, see. I think in all the time I have been artisting here, I have bought wood twice. One was a dollar sixty-two and the other was eighty cents. . . . Ben was always interested. His first words were: 'What are you doing, Lou?' And he'd come in and look at it, or I'd take it over to his house and ask him for an opinion. And he always had time, always had time. . . ."

Lou must be in his middle seventies now. He is one retired accountant who has plenty to do. Every day, if the weather is half-way decent, he and his wife stride along our streets, taking their exercise. Vigorously. The rest of the time he makes art. Good or bad, who cares. Once in a while he sells a piece; the rest accumulates.

"For the first time, since I retired, I have a feeling of freedom," he says. "I do something I really want to do, see, and I don't even have to sell it, it's mine. . . . Like the two Jews who meet and one of them says: 'I got so much money I can buy you and sell you.' And the other guy says: 'I got even more. I can buy you and keep you.'

"Ben really opened that door for me. He said: 'Put it on a bench and cut it.'"

Sara, Lou's wife, isn't going to be left behind. She paints little careful oils, mostly still lifes.

By the end of the fifties the town with its petty internal wars and small intimate gratifications must have become for Ben not so much a place to live as a place to come back to. He paid less and less attention to town affairs. The furies of the Board of Education or the Borough Council bored him now. He had moved out of range; he had better things to work on. And the town knew it and tacitly admitted it. The fish had grown too big for the pond.

As one middle-aged son of a cloak-maker put it: "Ben was the monument in the park."

The occasion of the twenty-fifth anniversary of the town's founding brought him back once more, but this time in all of his oversize dimension.

"It's a crime," he told a select group of us whom he had called together, "that in the United States there isn't a single memorial to Roosevelt, except maybe in Hyde Park. The British have got one. We don't. Not anywhere. What better place to start than in this place that wouldn't have existed if it wasn't for him?"

Earlier, if I remember correctly, the Borough Council in its wisdom had proposed to mark the occasion with a hot dog picnic: it would cost next to nothing; the nearby dairies made a practice of donating supplies for such minor municipal celebrations.

Hot dogs for history? Ben's love-hate for the town rose to the surface like a suppressed belch. If the Borough Council hadn't got itself involved in cut-price glory, he might never have resurrected the little scale model of the memorial from the closet where it had been accumulating layers of brown dust since it had been regretfully put away some fifteen years ago. Whether they liked it or not, he was going to pull the somnolent townspeople out of their shopkeeper's mentality. They were capable of more than that; they'd better be. And if the project he had decided on was obviously far too big for their skinny pockets, there were other ways of making them contribute.

What an organizer he turned out to be! First he called us in, singly or in twos or threes and showed us through the model and brought to bear on each one the whole complex of his powers: his enthusiasm, his hold on our affections, his fame (by implication rather than direct reference), his stupendous energy; and, where applicable, the irresistible pressure of our loyalty to the fading ideals we had once held close and inviolate under the umbrella of the New Deal. It would have been useless to resist him; any reservations he brushed off like flies.

By the time he called the first organizing meeting at his

home, he had involved at least one typical member of every section of the community. He divided us into working committees. He got eleven of us to sign as incorporators and saw to it that money given to his project was going to be tax-exempt. He fought with our local architect over every detail of the planned structure. And he commissioned his son Jon (who was just a youngster then) to make a foot-high plaster model of Roosevelt's head.

The Borough Council never had a chance. Ben packed the meeting hall with his troops and shamed the councilmen into making the first major contribution, one thousand dollars from the public treasury. It must have caused them physical pain, since they were used to turning over every dime three times before they spent it; but how could they resist this bull-headed visionary who had no patience with counting homes and figuring out how much the property tax would be increased on each one of them? By invoking FDR and the New Deal he had closed off all counter-argument. To oppose him effectively would have required that an elected representative impugn the very myth of the town's origins that was essential to its identity. And, of course, Ben knew this very well and smiled and waited confidently for the vote. The hot dog picnic was not mentioned again.

Ben demonstrated what leadership can do: he forced the town to surpass itself. The design was carried out by the young local architect, under some protest and with deep resentment of Ben's fatherly interference—but effectively. Myron Weiss was roped in as contractor. And Jon began to model the huge clay head in a garage in Boston. An elegant brochure was locally produced and sent out to a meticulously assembled list of presumably loaded individuals who could be counted on to recall the New Deal with affection. Every assigned job, except the actual printing of the brochure and the casting of the head in bronze, was done by local individuals or groups, no mean accomplishment for a community of a few hundred souls.

And the money started to flow in, in dribs and drabs at first, then gradually in larger checks. Ben went out of town and clubbed his affluent friends, collectors of his work, and such public figures as were indebted to him or the New Deal into giving more than they had any idea of giving. And imperceptibly the memorial became plausible even to those who had laughed at it as fantasy, and pride circulated through town like accelerated blood.

The ground-breaking ceremony on a hot summer day was an undiluted success. Old residents who had moved away years before sat on the grass with those who had remained while orators strung together the obligatory platitudes. You could sense the excitement in the crowd; a lost cohesion was temporarily regenerated. It wasn't hard to feel the spirit of Benjamin Brown in the furrowed faces of the homesteaders and their wives. It was a brutally hot day, and the ladies fanned themselves energetically with programs as their grandchildren crawled over their thickened legs embroidered with blue varicose veins. It was very rural and very Jewish and very American. It was folk art in the flesh.

From then on things went more smoothly than anyone had a right to expect. (Although, of course, feuds developed between individuals in the best tradition of the town.) The unpretentious brick amphitheatre grew around the reflecting pool. Jon accompanied the five-foot-high monumental head to Italy to be cast in bronze: when it came back, it looked unbelievably enormous. It was duly installed on a high marble-sheathed pedestal under a nave of tall, beautiful trees. Publicity was sent out, invitations were issued, speakers were recruited; lights were installed, microphones connected, a food service contracted on the parking lot in front of Murray Greenbaum's store. National and international attention became certain when Eleanor Roosevelt agreed to come. It was as if a searchlight had been turned on the insignificant set of houses in the Jersey fields.

On the day of the inauguration the town was full of state police from early morning on. Road signs pointed to us from telegraph poles all the way back to the turnpike. The Hightstown High School band, splendiferous in blue-and-white uniforms, arrived early and practiced nervously *in situ;* mothers of small flower girls made last-minute alterations on fluffy dresses; and Sam Morgenstern, the master of ceremonies, bustled, gimlet-eyed and sweating, from one end of the extraordinary operation (which looked thoroughly precarious at that point) to the other.

He needn't have worried. There were no hitches of any consequence. In due time the speakers and dignitaries arrived, the

128

governor of New Jersey, assorted stage personalities and literary lights, and Mrs. Roosevelt. They were given lunch at the Shahn home in the presence of a selection of local egos and a small delegation of original settlers. For these retired tailors the experience of being in the same room with the wife of the legendary president was more than unforgettable: it was dreamlike and utterly unimaginable in any framework of reality they could believe.

The ceremony went off beautifully. The weather was fine. The high school band did itself proud. Speaker followed speaker in an atmosphere much more formal than at the ground-breaking: after all, the TV networks were there, with their bored technicians snaking their cables through the crowd and every so often turning their cameras on the audience. But when Mrs. Roosevelt got up to speak of the great man with whom so many of us had died a little and whose bronze portrait head (dappled with leaf shadows) now looked over and past us immutably into the distance, emotion broke through and reserve was forgotten and people cried for their own past gentled by remembrance and for their own time of near-greatness that had somehow been mislaid over the years.

It was a grand event. It was a collective orgasm. And it was the last occasion, as far as I can see, when the town came together to be once more, at least in spirit, what it had originally been designed to be.

13

Before the summer was over, an unknown delinquent
broke off the three-hundred-dollar valve that had sent such a
pretty jet of water curving up from the middle of the reflecting
pool. By the time the fall had come and gone and the trees were
naked, the pool itself had stopped reflecting: a green slime was
mucking up the bottom, and the tiles were clogged with leaves
and tin cans and sandwich wrappers. After the first winter sad-
looking cracks were beginning to open in the brick tiers of the
amphitheatre.

The trouble was that we didn't really need an amphitheatre.
Maybe once or twice a year there might be a recital by a folk
singer; Pete Seeger performed once, I believe, for a cause, civil
rights or peace, I don't remember.

Or an overblown lady from Israel (resembling closely one of
our local mommas in an Ohrbach's gown) might be imported by
the Pioneer Women to sing Hebrew songs many of us couldn't
understand.

Of course there was always the annual eighth grade graduation. You could bet that for this occasion the pool was going to be
scrubbed and all the lights were going to be made to work and
our best piano was going to be lugged over from the school. And
everybody hoped it wasn't going to rain. Because on that evening
the auditorium was certain to be jammed, with standees against

the glowing sky, to watch a few girls in long white dresses and a few boys in dark suits go stiffly through the ritual they had been practicing for weeks under the massive bronze head.

But that was hardly enough. Even though—every once in a while—a band of very young and earnest students of instruments designed to make music took it into their collective heads that they should perform at the memorial. They couldn't begin to fill the place: only parents and the inveterately civic-minded were able to endure the heavy-footed stomping of the easier semiclassics.

The town was simply too small to generate an adequate demand for several hundred seats.

And so, gradually, the memorial was left alone, except for the children who liked to eat their lunch there and to play catch over its empty levels and to ride bikes along the curving paths through the plantings of pin oaks and dogwoods that weren't growing very well (with no one to help them) on the surrounding grounds. No doubt the children knew that the big, benign head had something to do with a dead president. They knew it as they knew hundreds of facts that were forever thrust at them in school and that had no reality to them whatever.

Sometimes it seemed as though the great head were trying to retreat under the canopy of tall trees behind it. It was being slowly blanked out as thousands of bronze likenesses are blanked out in parks and squares all over the world. FRANKLIN DELANO ROOSEVELT was incised in the marble underneath: IN HOMAGE. The chaste elegant letters were filled in with genuine gold leaf. The gold leaf must have intrigued some of the children, what with gold having such a big mystique about it; and when nobody was looking, they dug some of it out. I can just imagine their disappointment when they saw the tiny pile of shining dust in their dirty little hands. But I am not at all sure that they could have told you afterwards what the letters said. Anyway, eventually the inscription was regilded and it hasn't been disturbed since. Whoever had scratched it off in the first place must have learned that nothing was to be gained—what came out wasn't enough to be kept. And so now the head is simply part of the anonymity of the place everybody in town has come to call The Memorial when they talk about it at all. For all practical purposes the bronze head has shed its connection with the life that is going on every day. It has become something like a tree stump or a rock that has been there a very long time. It can be sat under or played around, but it has no given or proper name anymore, especially for the young to whom it is only one fragment in the abstraction history becomes to anyone who wasn't around when it happened.

You could divide the town into two parts: those who remembered and those who will never know. And together they had to coinhabit, with as much tolerance as they could muster, their near-identical house boxes left over from a vanished purpose.

In an interval no longer than a dozen years we had to come to some sort of terms with crisis piled on crisis. After the trauma of Korea we were clouted by the Cuban confrontation, followed, before we caught our breath, by the assassination of a president and, the next day, the murder of the supposed murderer: both televised live, transported instantaneously into our living rooms (while we were eating a sandwich, maybe) by that tyrannical electronic tube—the second shooting in unbearable close-up, an ordinary man, more astounded than terrified, dying while we watched. And Watts, Newark, Detroit exploding before our eyes, cities burning, split open by hatred . . . We couldn't encompass such a parade of enormities. And a lot of us went numb.

The climax came with the killing of King. This town had sent its old and young to the Washington march and had shared in his dream, as he gave voice to it. The civil rights movement was almost as healing to us as the great war had been: we could belong to it and expiate secret guilts all at the same time. And when this man King was shot, there was deep shock in town and real sorrow. The ceremony in his memory, hurriedly organized after his murder, crowded the memorial as no get-together before or since has been able to do.

At that very meeting we got the signal—unmistakably—that the end of King was going to be also the end of the last shred of hope that America was on the way to becoming the country we had believed it could be: that's what was ahead of us, black or white, was not a march toward a common dream, but a tearing and blind hating beyond the control of instrumentalities and certainly beyond us, bumbling along from day to day in our power-less village.

A local man we had thought of as our friend, a roly-poly brown man with his mat of wooly hair trimmed short about his round face, stood up in front of the great bronze head, and cried a despairing fury at us. It far exceeded any anger we had thought he could contain. He had been playing the role of the good fellow since he moved in with his pretty Irish wife. He was always full of jokes; we had eaten bagels and cream cheese with this comfort-able armchair of a man and drunk with him socially at his house or ours; we had forgotten that he was a Negro. And here, sud-denly, there was nothing jolly about his fat anymore. It quivered with rage as he accused us, as though we were the ones who had pressed the trigger of the rifle. He all but called us racists for merely existing. He shoved our genuine grief down our throats and told us we had no right to it.

"Look around," he shouted, "in the rural slum all around your clean, safe town! See how black people live! What have you done about it?"

He shocked some of us enough to make us look into our-selves and question: what could *we* do about it? He made a lot of us squirm and switch angers: what had *he* done about it? What gave him the privilege of hectoring us? The fact that he was black?

Few seemed to understand even on reflection how much it must have hurt him to reject us whom he had for so long been trying to join, and that this was the root of his violence.

The story spread that, after the news of the assassination came over the TV, he had sat all night in a corner of his house with a shotgun on his knees, glowering at his white wife and halfwhite kids. Maybe so; maybe not. The important thing is not what he did, but that the rumor had so suddenly become believ-able. King's murderer had accomplished exactly what he had set out to accomplish: as far away as this irrelevant community there wasn't going to be a wealth of forgiveness on either side of the color line for decades to come.

There was a girl in town (a plump, small-featured blonde girl with baby-blue eyes and freckles) who had gone down South to work for civil rights. She was brilliant in her college work, as such things are measured. And this, no doubt, pleased her parents who prided themselves on their well-tempered radicalism, the old-fashioned kind that dated back to the thirties. Her father is a small executive in a big conglomerate, and her mother teaches grammatical English to the young of the underprivileged, to whom it is a language as foreign as French.

No doubt the prospect of a fourteen-carat intellectual in the family fulfilled hopes in them they may not even have known they had. It must have come hard to them to let her go. What nightmares did they suffer watching the eleven o'clock news? After all, people were getting killed down there.

But at this late stage in their lives they couldn't suddenly deny the way they saw themselves and hoped she saw them also. And so she went.

And here she came back, licked. Not by hoodlums, not by the power structure personified in some bull of a sheriff: but by the very blacks for whom she had risked so much.

"Go home," they so much as told her, "and work on your own people. This is our fight."

With the summer only half over, she wandered through our streets, sullen, taciturn, her eyes on the ground as if she were looking for a lost earring. I'm told she did a lot of crossword puzzles till it was time to return to school, to whatever it represented.

I don't know whether she ever forgave the town (or her parents) for having allowed her to go out, filled with ideas that didn't work anymore. . . . She never comes here if she can help it. She finished college with honors, I understand, then took a law degree. Along the way she got married to another anguished intellectual and moved to the opposite end of the country, to the West Coast, as far away as possible. If she's doing anything out there with her law that has a meaning we could understand, I haven't heard of it.

She is, of course, not the only one of our young people who left our certitudes and who say no to our yesses. A lot of them didn't have to leave town: they undressed themselves of us right here in plain sight of the neighbors. Some dig for reassurance in old, discredited mysteries, and one or two actually go for consolation to the Ouija board. A few hide in drugs. And some just float. They are quite impossible to talk to. For us.

The heritage of FDR simply isn't pertinent anymore.

In the good old days of poverty a respectable progressive was pro-union and pro-Negro as a matter of course. It wouldn't have occurred to him that the two could conflict. But the New York teachers' strike took care of that: it made the distinction sharp and hard.

On one side were the teachers (the Jews) and on the other side were the blacks (the anti-Semites). This was how the press and the TV handled the issue. And this was pretty much how it was understood here, not just by people who liked their answers simple, but reluctantly, painfully by many of the more sophisticated, who were pulled by their roots away from what they had thought of as their principles and who discovered remnants of tribal loyalty in themselves that surprised them. And this included nearly everybody old enough to recall the time when issues were nice and clear.

It was a most uncomfortable time.

14

It is hard to say who died first, old Louis Rosenzweig (Goldie's husband, who wasn't really so old) or the Four-H Club. Both were retired by a time that wasn't theirs anymore: the Jewish, European-bred socialist and the long-established very American organization designed to teach the kids of frontier farmers the rugged virtues: thrift and calf-raising, independence and baking pies and making your own clothes and canning home-grown vegetables.

Louis died blessedly, swiftly among his flowers. The Four-H lingered, with periods of remission, then withered and finally faded out for lack of interest.

Our children might play in the fields and woods, but not one of them wanted to be a farmer. They knew too much about farming, they saw it all around them: the family-run chicken farms, squeezed till they had to quit by mechanized egg factories, and the farmers themselves, bent crooked by the fiercely hard work demanded of them by the soil and the fluctuations of the market. Our children didn't dream of driving tractors when they grew up—they hoped to drive MGs or Corvettes. (This was, of course, before the revulsion of the suburban young against materialism, technological stultification and the work clock built into the suckers who supported them.)

Louis Rosenzweig was the first to go of the incorporators of the memorial to Franklin Delano Roosevelt. Louis was missed. The Four-H wasn't. Not enough for volunteers to take on the job of running it.

Volunteers of all kinds were getting hard to find. It was even becoming difficult to dig up candidates to run for public office. Most of the elections were uncontested since almost nobody was willing to endure the abuse and drudgery of the endless meetings that seemed to be required to run the school and the town. The older people felt they'd done their share, and the new arrivals—if they stayed long enough to qualify—had more agreeable things to do with their energy. Many of them followed national fads pretty closely: they went in for cookouts and long skiing weekends in upper New York State and as far away as Vermont. What a change!

The PTA too showed signs of terminal neglect. Ten years earlier it was still viable enough to make a hundred paid-up members go hysterical over the election of a president as though it were a race for national office instead of a mild auxiliary to a school distinguished mainly by its smallness. At least then the citizens were still capable of small-town passion, and our institutions, such as they were, hadn't yet begun to smell of mold.

The national spending ritual (it was a sin not to go into hock) that accompanied the beginning of full-scale slaughter in Southeast Asia, was doubling the number of cars in town. Most houses had at least two parked in the driveway, since a lot of garages were jammed with retired but not yet quite discarded furniture, decrepit appliances, rusty bicycles, snow tires and self-propelled lawn mowers, or, in the younger set, power tools and motorcycles. This same paper prosperity was responsible for the sudden appearance of swimming pools all over town. In the space of a few years three swim clubs and half a dozen private pools were built. The filtering and chlorination of our water (which has an exceptionally high iron content) became a subject of earnest discussion at the store.

The turquoise-colored holes in the ground, surrounded by aluminum garden chairs, began multiplying immediately after the battle of the town pool. If somebody had tried to open a house of prostitution, he could have whipped up no greater indignation than the well-meaning group which thought it could convince the town to build a community pool. They were, for the most part, naive dreamers: they visualized a regular country club—you know, tennis courts, a children's playground . . . Not right away, you understand; start with the pool, they thought, the rest will come later.

Well, it didn't come at all. No part of it. It was voted down. The fight before the referendum was memorable, as violent as the ruckus that tore the town apart when a teacher was fired on suspicion of homosexuality. It was strange. You would think that a town where a co-operative past was commonly given lip service would overwhelmingly support a community swimming pool; but you would think so only if you conveniently forgot how all the co-ops had failed.

In the swimming pool war there was no way of predicting who was going to be shooting at whom and from which side. The old labels didn't seem to have their usual meanings. Left-wingers and right-wingers were freely mixed. In the meetings and in private only the forty or so remaining pensioners could be counted on with certainty: they were broke and scared of more taxes. But by themselves they were helpless. Their only weapon was the appeal of their weakness.

Not that they were united. Howard Novick could easily have been on their side; he was old enough. Instead he made a cause of the community pool. He drew up the plans. He collected data and pamphlets from all sorts of state agencies and as far away as Washington: what could be done and how it should be done to get the best result for the least money. He did his homework diligently, as he did everything, for he was a painstaking man. (Howard is a writer and a sculptor in wood, a little didactic and given to long, learned discourse, and without enemies under normal circumstances.) And here, all of a sudden, he was attacked, maligned, insulted by individuals he had thought of warmly as neighbors for years. Why? Why, for God's sake?

He's been puzzling about it ever since.

"Whatever I came up with was wrong," he says. "The design

was wrong, the size was too small, my cost estimates were ridiculous. . . . I know now that reason had nothing to do with it. . . ."

The attacks were irrational, no doubt about that. A public swimming pool in Roosevelt, of all places! Quite likely, the old terror of the outsider was again hidden under the antagonism. How, it was asked, could you keep people out? Before you knew it, there were going to be all kinds of white trash driving into town, parking on our streets: undesirables from Perrineville and Clarksburg. . . . Pools were all right in Florida where the climate called for them, or, for that matter, in Princeton where the swells lived. A lot of our people still saw a swimming pool as one of those superfluous luxuries the rich put on their estates. We didn't want any part of such ostentation. And—the old question again—who was going to pay for the upkeep?

Just before the vote on the referendum Daniel Loeb sent around a flyer. Let the supporters of the community pool keep their hands out of the taxpayers' pockets, he wrote. But then Dan had always been a rough man in a fight. Any fight, no matter how trivial.

Dan did as much as anybody to defeat the pool. He was an active small-town politician with a gift for the deep cut, the lasting injury. His bluntness was proverbial as was his honesty. He took it upon himself to go from house to house cajoling, arguing, threatening bankruptcy, awakening half-forgotten apprehensions. It worked. The community pool was stopped cold. And almost immediately pool clubs and private pools proliferated. Probably this was exactly what Dan wanted. Because he was a remarkable hater, a dour personality, and he was able to keep a resentment simmering longer, I think, than anyone else in this environment of expert resenters.

"I'll be damned," I remember him saying to me at the time, "if I want to swim in the same water with the Pinkuses. Talk to them at the post office, all right. Swim with them, not on your life. . . ."

I wouldn't be surprised if Dan had a pint of bile stored up in him from the time when he was on the Borough Council or the Board of Education, and when the Pinkus clan needled him and gave him a hard time. And he wasn't going to go soft at this late date and miss the chance to pay them back.

Dan then was still cutter for a high-class dress house in Manhattan. He took pride in his craft, and to him it was worth spending twenty years playing pinochle on the commuter train. That train, for him and his cronies, must have been like a *Stammtisch* for the regular customers of a beer hall, so that he didn't mind driving twelve miles to the railroad station before seven in the morning. For twenty years—longer than anyone else could stand it—he spent nearly four hours daily (when the train was on time) getting to his job and back. He never complained.

Dan was a tree of a man, built to fit the size of his antipathies. Everything about him was big, his frame, his nose and his dark, liquid, beautiful eyes which looked straight at you out of purple sockets from under black eyebrows and a mass of black hair. Anytime he wanted to, he could scare almost everybody simply by scowling; his voice and his heavy sarcasm and his well-known inflexibility of mind made people think twice before they crossed him.

Yet—not being more of a piece than anybody else—Dan was a warm and even indulgent family man. I can only judge by externals. I don't know what went on in the house, though he and his tiny, busy wife and his son and two daughters lived not far from us for many years. Anytime there was the slightest reason, Dan's women were suddenly endowed with slinky gowns that actresses would pay a mint for. The wedding of the younger daughter was a bash which is still talked about—catered under a multicolored tent, with literally hundreds of guests, locals and out-of-towners; the ladies in long creations bedecked with sequins, the men in the sort of summer whites and resplendent blazers seen normally only at Grossinger's or in the men's wear supplement of the *New York Times*. The liquor and cigar bill alone must have cost a couple of months of Dan's salary.

Dan believed in doing things right. And his idea of the right way was determined by his tastes. His notion of a Saturday's entertainment consisted of driving to a shopping center near Camden where some sixty stores and shops under the same enormous roof spread neon, Muzak and glamour over broad avenues crowded with families and flowering plants. Dan told me repeatedly how beautiful it was. He spoke of it as a Californian might speak of Yosemite. You didn't have to buy anything, just looking was enough.

Dan was a combination of a kind of innocent wonder at the slick miracle of American rich-bitchiness in full production, and a hard, shrewd, utterly pragmatic outlook he had been taught on the concrete of a city in depression. Out of this mixture he had distilled a very rigid set of standards—a kind of prickly integrity. And it was this integrity, as much as anything, which eventually, when the circumstances were finally favorable, brought him together with Ben Shahn in an unlikely, deeply emotional friendship.

The building of the Roosevelt Memorial supplied the opportunity. Nostalgia for the New Deal—the early New Deal—provided a meeting ground: in the memories of both men it was the last time when practically anything at all looked possible. It was a consensus between them, who had little else in common to start with.

Dan accepted the job of business manager. He gave himself wholly to it, every moment of free time till all hours of the night. He took on all the essential trivia Ben detested: the schedules, the disposition of moneys, bills, deposits, payments and the bulk of the arrangements for activities to raise funds locally. Most important, he could be relied on to remember what Ben would surely have forgotten. And he had far more staying power than Ben's intellectual familiars.

And gradually each found in the other, I imagine, qualities to admire and strengths to lean on; and over the next few years they shared an affection, almost a tenderness, that went well beyond the usefulness of the painter of pictures to the cutter of gowns (whose best friends up to this point had been an egg dealer and a junkman on the way to making it big).

And then, one day, Dan's heart gave out and within a week he was dead.

Even those who had it in for Dan were sorry. A voice had been drowned—a growl of a voice, if you like, with a threat of a bite in it. But voices like that were becoming rare in Roosevelt.

With Dan gone, who was there left to push against, who wasn't worn out or venal?

His dying was so unexpected. Dan couldn't have been much over fifty-five. I can just imagine some of our older citizens feeling themselves all over for unexplained bumps, examining their tongues in the bathroom mirror and cutting down on their smoking for a couple of weeks.

I guess we all winced a little under the cold breath on the back of our necks.

In keeping with tradition people brought gifts of food to the family during the first couple of weeks. Then Dan's daughters returned to their husbands and the boy to his school. And the widow stayed for a while in the empty house till she wasn't able to stand it anymore and rented it to a furniture salesman who wanted to be a writer, a Jewish boy with an Italian wife and two kids. The couple broke up soon after they arrived, and now the wife lives alone with the children, and the husband comes to visit the children once a week, and all of them are separately miserable in the house that used to be Dan's.

Ben wept when Dan went out like a switched-off light. Ben wept much more easily than people knew. They knew his laughter and his anger; he kept his weeping private. But who am I to say whom he wept for, Dan or himself?

I have an idea that Ben had been observing his own slow dying in a sort of awful fascination for a long time, and that Dan's death served to confirm his panic. After all, he was going on seventy. He could see and feel the waning of his powers better than anybody, and this enraged him and frightened him: there was still so much he had to do.

"He wasn't ready," Stella says. "He was a young man trapped in the tragedy of being old. Some people are ready. Some people are good and sick of it. But not Ben. Maybe he would have been ready at ninety. Ready, for a man like Ben, is when you have no strong needs left to imprint on the world. . . ."

He was working steadily, without letup, even after his right leg started to give him trouble, and he had to use a cane to get around. (There were three or four canes leaning against a carved wooden monster from Bali he had installed in the vestibule.)

For some time his work had been changing. He had given up on the small authentic detail he used to place cunningly among his bold forms to draw the viewer in. He'd stopped caring about relevance. What he was after now was myth—Greek myth, Hebrew myth, medieval Christian myth; and in dealing with the present, he tried to raise its image to the level of the mythical—simplified, pared down, taller and heavier than life. Bernarda claims that he changed after reading Jung. Maybe. Whatever the origin of his new direction, I think he was striving for survival, for the quality that could outlive a man, for a hedge against mortality.

He kept his dread well chained. But every so often it would break out—at the most inconvenient moment, especially when he was about to give a speech at some sort of public function. And he would start to sweat, and a weakness would come over him, and he had to sit down quickly to avoid fainting. Then, after a short interval, the terror receded and he was able to go on with the business at hand almost as if nothing had happened. But something had happened. And he knew it.

It was a battle between the weakening flesh that couldn't last much longer and a stubborn spirit that couldn't give in. He developed diabetes. He had a heart attack. When his daughter Suzy was dying far away in London, he had to let Bernarda fly over there without him. His doctor wouldn't let him go. That was when I saw him weep endlessly, brokenly, for days.

"The Jews have a saying," he told me then, "that there is no worse punishment than to survive your own child."

He had never been a doting Jewish father. He was too busy working to pay much attention to his kids. When his mind was free and he felt like it, he could be a warm and wise and stimulating parent; most of the time he was concentrated elsewhere, inside himself, and then he could be abrupt and capricious and unjust. Still, I think that he really started dying after Suzy's kidney failed in England, where she had fled, I do believe, to put as much distance as she could between herself and her outsize father.

Ben limped around town on his cane for a while longer. Then he gave up walking. He grew a beard, which matched his wispy white hair and made him look more like a well-trimmed

Santa Claus than one of the prophets. He spent his evenings in an armchair in front of the TV set.

He still fought. He designed full-page ads against the war in Vietnam that were published in the *New York Times*. He made violent posters against Goldwater. But his heart wasn't in it. Not like it used to be.

"In the last couple of years he was really quite a different person," Stella says. "I think he was far more depressed and upset than anybody knew. I think it's a measure of his courage and dignity that people didn't know. But I had that terrible feeling that he was increasingly vulnerable and it saddened me terribly when even Ben began to get quiet and less contentious. It was very sad to see somebody like him too vulnerable to fight back. . . ."

But the town did know or at least it sensed what was happening in the Shahn house. People would ask after Ben, and they would keep their voices low as if he could hear them. Even his enemies.

Eventually he was taken to the hospital in Princeton and a couple of weeks later to a bigger, fancier hospital in New York; and he couldn't hide it anymore—from himself or others—that he was deathly sick. But even in the hospital he refused to capitulate, he still tried to work. On the day before they operated on his cancer, he insisted on completing the signing of his last edition of prints. And two days later he was gone.

A few out-of-towners came to the funeral. The earth was yellow where it had been dug up next to Suzy's grave, whose body had been shipped back from her refuge abroad to be interred in the soil she had run away from when she was alive. Ben's dealer was in attendance, and so was the lawyer who was going to be the executor of his estate; and the family, of course, and a handful of close friends and such local people as felt called upon to make the short, muddy trip to the cemetery. It wasn't a big funeral.

An old gentleman—a specialist in civil rights law—pronounced the eulogy. It wasn't the usual laudatory tripe, the man really meant what he was saying. You could tell he was genuinely moved, and what he said went to the core of what some of us were feeling. An insurance agent who is famous for his knowledge of the ancient melodies sang something in Hebrew: unaccompanied, the lonely falsetto spread out from him over the knot of silent people (black as crows in their winter overcoats, with their collars turned up against the cold) and faded on the air.

And we went home and began the hard long work of learning to live with the hole in ourselves that was all we had left of Ben.

At first it seemed as though nothing were changed very much in Roosevelt. Except at the store and the post office where Ben's absence was unmistakable. Within a year the town began to realize that something more was lacking than another resident who had grown old and died, as people will anywhere, in the normal course of passing time.

One day I ran into Si, and he came over to the house for a cup of coffee and we talked about Ben.

"In the last couple of years Ben became important to me," Si said. "He really did. I didn't have my father to talk to. Even when my father was alive—you know, most young people can't talk to their parents . . . I'm not an outgoing guy. I don't have many close friends. I don't know if there are twelve people in the whole world I really like. But Ben was one of those few people. We had a *Gemütlichkeit*. It wasn't put on. If it had been put on I would have sensed it. . . .

"I think Roosevelt is dead with his death. Roosevelt will die. I think Ben was Roosevelt and Roosevelt was Ben. This town's value is not in the houses and the roads and the facilities we have. Roosevelt has meaning only because of its people, because of the feelings of these people and the interests of these people. And Ben was influential in bringing a lot of these people to Roosevelt. . . .

"I think Roosevelt is dead but doesn't know it. The only reason it's not buried is because it hasn't started to stink yet. But that will happen too. . . ."

15

Roosevelt is not dead. Towns don't die that easily. But there have been changes (which might look like signs of failing, if you want to see them that way) in the two years since this chronicle was started.

We have lost a center. Murray Greenbaum had to sell the store. He couldn't compete with the Shop-Rite in Hightstown. Now a liquor store is going broke in the same location. We don't drink enough. And who wants to gossip in a repository of cut-rate whisky and cheap wine?

The Volunteer Fire Company languishes. There are not enough men around during the day. And the First Aid Squad is reduced to accepting women.

The price of houses has gone from seventeen thousand to twenty-five thousand dollars. New homes are being built, and they look like strangers who have lost their way. They go for thirty thousand and up.

Five miles away in Hightstown ten crosses were burned by the Ku Klux Klan reconstituted; outside agitators, of course. Nobody here seemed to worry too much. The target, this time, was clearly not Jewish: it was black.

Only one black family remains in town.

The size of the real estate developments creeping toward us is unbelievable.

The Fourth of July is shrinking. Few flags and hardly any parades. With the Vietnam war still going on and on, we have no stomach for celebrations. Except for weddings and Bar Mitzvahs: they can be as gaudy as ever.

Divorces multiply among the young. Some of the ex-husbands, deprived of bed and board, are sleeping in the cemetery on warm summer nights.

Somebody is building a house so big it needs two lots to stand on. It's an outlander: it's not bad-looking and it would be all right in Princeton. In this town it brags. It is supposed to have five bathrooms. People refer to it as The Roosevelt Hilton.

Our main street has been incorporated in a direct road to the shore. Cars and trucks slam through it at fifty miles an hour: it's too much for our part-time cop.

The traditional unity fades: the old drink, the young smoke, and each disapproves of the other.

Whole classes in school don't have a single Jewish child in them.

The old are getting older. Myron's legs are wobbly. He can't work as he used to. For me he's still our poet laureate.

Yetta has died.

But the town is alive. It's going somewhere, though I couldn't tell you where it's bound. I can feel the vibrations of the engine. It isn't going to be Benjamin Brown's town or Ben Shahn's town. In time it may forget both of them. But by some mysterious process quite beyond my understanding, the quality of what they tried for in this place is still here, however faintly, under all the progress. Or perhaps I just think so. Because I want to believe it.

ROOSEVELT, NEW JERSEY
is published on the Tenth Anniversary
of Grossman Publishers, June 18th, 1972.

The text has been composed on the
Linotype in Granjon.
The display type is Goudy Heavyface.
The book has been printed by letterpress
on 70 lb. Antique paper.
Composed, printed, and bound by H. Wolff
Manufacturing Company, Inc., New York.
Designed by Jacqueline Schuman.

WITHDRAW.